# INVEnsE

*A grumpy man's guide to life in verse*

*A collection of poems
mingled with personal anecdotes
by Peter Bacon*

*All text and pictures copyright © Peter Bacon 2019*

*Peter Bacon has asserted his right to be identified as the author of this work in accordance with the Coyright, Designs and Patent Act 1988.*

*All rights reserved. No part of this publication may be reproduced, stored in a retrieval system or transmitted in any form or by any means, electronic, mechanical, photocopying, recording or otherwise, without the prior permission of the copyright owner.*

*inversepoems@gmail.com*

*Kindle Direct Publishing, an Amazon.com company*

*ISBN: 9781090400130*


*Technological changes happen so quickly nowadays.*

*Things we might have thought impossible
even fifty years ago are happening right now.
You never know!*

# When pigs can fly

When £10 notes can grow on trees,
When erupting lava starts to freeze,
When a square peg fits inside a round hole,
When sabre-tooth tigers roam the North Pole.

When archaeologists declare they've found the missing link,
When you can lead a horse to water *and* can make it drink,
When a pig sprouts wings and learns to fly,
*Then* - the price of bacon will be sky high.

# Acknowledgements

*Cartoon illustrations
by Brian Sage*

*Poems, photographs, paintings
and other illustrations by Peter Bacon
except those poems marked BS/PB
for which Brian and Peter
should be blamed equally.*

*With thanks to my wife Tiz
for encouragement, proof-reading
and for being the inspiration
for some of the poems and also
to Colin Bunyan for his
positive suggestions.*

# Contents

## FAMILY LIFE

Wake up, get out of bed ........ 7

Standing in the shower ......... 8

For better or verse  BS/PB ...... 10

My love .................... 15

The TV weather girl ............ 16

Pardon my spilling .............. 17

Archie's visit  BS/PB ................ 18

Barbed thoughts
from a home .......................... 20

Cuddly toys and friends ..... 22

The countryside ................... 24

You couldn't get better
in a restaurant ....................... 25

The ballad of
Buzz and Roo ........................ 27

Moving story ......................... 29

If you died first ..................... 34

## MODERN TIMES

The daily grind ..................... 36

What makes us English? ..... 38

Put the other person first .... 41

Jack and Jill ........................... 42

Have you been good? .......... 43

Min's reign
stops play  BS/PB ..................... 44

A hole in my bucket list ...... 49

Everyone speaks
English now .............................. 50

Plastic bag ................................ 52

Why is it
always the Vicar? ................. 53

Old woman ........................... 54

Children today ..................... 55

ATMs ..................................... 56

At the Garden Centre .......... 57

A sporting Valentine ............ 64

Goldilocks .............................. 66

You know my name ............. 67

The River Stour .................... 68

Common sense ..................... 70

## THE PLACE TO BE

It's a mystery ......................... 72

Go Min go! BS/PB .................. 74

A day on the river ................ 78

Aah York! ............................... 81

The yellow menace .............. 83

My perfect day ...................... 84

## TIMEFRAME

The maiden voyage of
The Silver Flash .................... 87

Red Rodgers .......................... 90

The waiting game ................ 93

A knight came a-riding ....... 94

Robin and a band
of outlaws ............................... 97

It's about time ....................... 99

The Silver Flash
flies again ............................. 100

Fray D'ah ............................. 104

Month after month ............ 107

The dragon & George ....... 114

The return of
The Silver Flash ..................117

## ON THE MOVE

Off the rails ......................... 122

Over the limit .................... 124

My fellow passengers ........ 126

I've got a new bike ............. 127

Cedric's special day ........... 129

The double door game ...... 133

Humpty and
Miss Muffet ......................... 134

An unexpected stop ........... 136

The coach trip ..................... 138

The day we went to see
The Flying Scotsman ......... 139

Cedric and Min
go to Clacton .......................... 142

## LOOKING BACK

The old days ....................... 148

No more ............................... 151

The WW2 Weekend ........... 152

Prime time ........................... 154

When Cedric
met Min BS/PB ..................... 156

On reflection ....................... 159

# FAMILY LIFE

*This book is full of my 'lightbulb moments' when I've felt the need to vent my feelings on various happenings and situations.*

*I've never been interested in poetry. I've always found it stuffy and difficult to get to grips with. I remember, when I was a schoolboy, that we had to learn poems by heart. The Lady of Shalott and The Rhyme of the Ancient Mariner come to mind. I can still just about recall the odd line . . . but that's all. However, I've always been fond of the poems recited by Stanley Holloway and more recently those of Pam Ayres.*

*I reached the age of fifty nine without writing any poetry of my own apart from a couple of soppy lines when I was courting but, now I've started, I can't stop. I wrote this first poem for my wife on our anniversary, inspired as I'm sure you'll realise by W. Wordsworth. Well, if he could do it . . .*

# Wake up, get out of bed

I wander lonely in a crowd that flows . . .
    "WAKE UP, GET OUT OF BED".
A suave imagined hero conquering all . . .
    "COME ON YOU SLEEPY HEAD".
Now gone, that half remembered world -
    it's back into reality I tread.

I lie cocooned, impossibly comfortable -
    but know that it can't last.
Duty calls - I stir myself - throw off the sheets -
    must now move fast!
I concentrate - what day is it? Check it's a workday -
    sit up straight,
Whilst from the kitchen, loud and clear,
    my conscience calls - must not be late.
Up already, she greets the day downstairs: my wife -
    my friend - my love - my better half - my mate.

I stumble to the bathroom, pray,
    get washed and dress,
Look in the mirror, comb, plump up, tease out my hair:
    it's still a mess!
Now to negotiate the stairs. I look outside:
    the weather's poor.
Another rainy day. Still, never mind,
    I turn and push the kitchen door.
And there she stands, the SUNSHINE of my life -
    who'd ask for more?

A vision of loveliness -
    'tis a sight for sore eyes.
Arms outstretched,
    I hurry in and claim my prize!

*My wife has been very patient with me and my funny little ways - one of which is my long showers. I only shower once a week but I'll then make up for all the water I've saved during the past six days. She's finally accepted that's what I do (well sort of).*

*Inspiration for a poem could come at the most unexpected times - like in the middle of the night or when I'm having a shower and, if I don't write it down right away, it's probably lost forever. So I might take a pen and a scrap of paper to the bedroom or even into the bathroom with me to scribble down the latest nonsense as soon as I get out.*

*Unfortunately, the paper might get a little soggy.*

# Standing in the shower

I'm in that place again where I can
        shut my eyes and drift away.
And for just a few brief moments,
        that's where I'm gonna stay.
Given half a chance, I'll linger here
        for half an hour,
Just standing in the shower.

I'm on some faraway island
        in a tropical storm, a castaway.
I'm underneath a gentle and warm waterfall,
        perhaps I'm just on holiday.
But, if I so desired, I could turn up the power,
Because, of course, I'm standing . . .
        I'm *still* standing in the shower.

I wash *all* my cares away. I shut my eyes
        and let the water beat down
On what hair I still retain upon my crown
And let it trickle down my face.
I'm in another time. I'm in another place.
I'm young and nubile once again.
        I don't look at my fat tum.
I'm in my prime. I'm thin. I'm 21!
I'm as slim as Nelson's column or The Burj Khalifa
        or The Shanghai Tower.
*No I'm not!* It's just another daydream -
        I'm *still* standing . . . *in the shower!*

And then a thought occurs -
        as I've been here for some time now - err . . .
That I should use the soap and shampoo,
        while I'm standing in the shower.
If I don't get a move on,
        my wife will get into a stew, no doubt.
I guess she might be wondering
        when on earth I'm coming out
But I've finished now - she needn't glower.
I'm not still standing in the shower

    . . . *not anymore!*

*Some marriages last for many years. Cedric and Minnie Fitzwilliam were now quite old and they'd often discuss the adventures they'd had during their many happy years together.*

*Their wedding day, for instance, had been anything but conventional.*

# For better or verse

Cedric and Min's wedding photo
Still hung on their wall in a frame.
Though the years had brought a few changes,
The two of them still felt the same.

The pair had been totally smitten
Since the time of their very first date.
They were married just
two short months later.
They didn't see why
they should wait.

Their parents both queried the hurry.
Was there something they had to explain?
Min said "There's no need to worry"
But Mum asked again . . . and again . . . and again.

The best man had already been chosen
By pulling his name from a hat.
Lo and behold, it was Algy -
Cedric's brother, and best pal, at that.

In actual fact he'd come second.
'Harris Tweed' was the first Cedric drew.
Min complained "You've pulled out the label.
Is that really the best you can do?"

They were pleased Algy's name had been picked.
After all, he's the reason they'd met.
He'd unwittingly 'ignited' their passion,
So, forever they'd be in his debt.

Min's bridesmaid was the ice cream girl,
Known in the cheap seats as Lollipop Lil.
She'd seen far too many James Bond films
And she joked she'd a 'licence to chill'.

At the pictures, old Tom was the doorman.
As 'first usher', he marshalled the queue.
He's the one who shouts "Ush in the cheap seats!"
After all, that's what ushers will do.

He'd stand just outside the black curtain,
Checking tickets of green, pink or blue
But, when he'd got Min's invitation,
Out of habit he'd torn it in two!

He'd enlisted the help of the vicar,
The clergy are dab-hands with glue -
Good at 'joinings-together' and 'unions'
And . . . of course . . . marriages too.

To honour the time of their meeting,
Their wedding took place late at night.
When Min entered, they blew out the candles
And the service continued by torchlight.

Walking backwards down the aisle with her father
Was another nice detail to add.
As an usherette Min found it easy,
Though the same can't be said for her dad.

He was enjoying the wedding
He'd spent all his day in the pub
But he'd blotted his copybook badly
Asking Min for a choc-ice or tub.

Relations 'tween both of the families
Had always been frosty, it's true.
Hostilities went back generations
Who started it, nobody knew.

Both sides of the aisle eyed each other.
The tension could be cut with a knife
But for now they just sat there and glowered
As the couple were named man and wife.

The wedding reception was awkward -
It got off to a very bad start
When a tipsy Mrs Fitzwilliam
Called Min 'nothing more than a tart'.

Though Min didn't usually swear,
An exception was made in this case.
The air was turned blue and paint blistered
As she put 'Mrs F' in her place.

To avoid any more confrontation
They were then kept apart, out of reach.
So things all calmed down and ran smoothly . . .
Till the best man's unfortunate speech.

He said the bridesmaids were *all* rather lovely,
He'd enjoyed the Champagne and the food
But those at the back couldn't hear him.
His praises all got misconstrued!

Had he just said the bridesmaids were UGLY?
And praised the CAMPAIGN and the FEUD?
They'd not stand for that at a wedding
And started to pelt him with food.

Then, like a shot from a rifle,
Poor Algy was sploshed in the face
By a well aimed portion of trifle,
Wrapped up in a napkin of lace.

That was the opening salvo.
The battle had really begun
When they brought up
the heavy artillery -
Fruit grenades and a
homemade machine bun.

Taking cover 'neath the tables
(with the Champers and the beer)
People cowered there for safety
Till they heard the last 'all clear'.

Older folk there were reminded
Of the 'spirit of the Blitz',
Singing all the Vera Lynn songs
Whilst avoiding direct hits.

Not wanting a part in the bunfight,
Cedric and Min slipped away.
They sat in the park feeling saddened.
An old squabble had ruined their day.

"Never mind" they agreed, "leave them to it
Let's go back now and say our goodbyes
We'll help clean the mess and say sorry"
But they were in for a lovely surprise . . .

For when they returned to the venue
They were welcomed and greeted with cheers.
Both sides had made up and were saying
"Best wedding we've been to in years".

All glasses were raised to the couple -
A 'cocktail' of Champagne and beers.
It had been an emotional wedding -
Even the cake was in tiers.

Since that day there'd been sunshine and showers,
With some ups and some downs like the weather
But that was the start of a lifetime of love -
Through it all, they'd been happy together.

As Cedric awoke from his daydream,
Min gave him a quizzical look.
They smiled as she carried on knitting
. . . and Cedric went back
to his book.

BS/PB

# My love

My love, she likes a red, red rose
And tulips, freesias - all of those.
She's not impressed by flashy cars,
       jewellery bling, expensive clothes -
Extra enhancements not required
       and she just needs a car that goes.
Shall I compare her to a summer's day?
       I *could* . . . I suppose.

*Weather forecasting is much more reliable nowadays. If the prediction is that it's going to rain, then it probably will. The male weather-forecasters on television usually look very smart in their dark three piece suits, the only colour emanating from a fairly muted tie.*

*However, if the forecaster happens to be female, I usually spend the whole of the weather forecast distracted by her appearance and as soon as it's finished I start to wonder what the weather will be like tomorrow!*

# The TV weather girl

The weather forecast has finished
    - and I'm *still* no wiser.
It's the weather girl's fault.
    *It's all down to her!*
I find I'm transfixed but don't hear what she says.
I don't look at the map . . . I couldn't care less.
My entire concentration's on the state of her hair
Or on what she's decided (or been told what) to wear.
That dress doesn't suit her – it's far, far too tight
And the colours all clash – they're too vivid, too bright.

I mimic how she moves her hand up and down.
I wonder, will she smile - will she wink? - will she frown?
Will she speak in a rush or a leisurely pace?
If she runs out of time will she then have to race?
There's one girl who shouts, the next one is husky
One girl's too thin, another's too busty.
Then there's all the information they feel they should share
About Europe or Siberia . . . but I don't *live* there!

Drift in the Atlantic, storms in America,
Isotopes, isobars, high or low pressure.
And then there's the Gulf Stream's new direction.
My head's spinning - there's just *too much* information.
Will we have rain? Will it be dry?
Don't blind me with science, I don't need to know why.
*"Stop showing off – I really don't care*
*I'm trying to discover what clothes I should wear!"*

I've just thought, if I stick paper on the left of the screen
And mute the sound, I might just glean
If it'll be hot or cold or wet or dry
Then again, I *could* go outside . . . *and look at the sky!*

*Typing has never been a strong point of mine. With the introduction of computers, I've had to teach myself how to do it and have managed to get to a reasonable speed - but still using just the two fingers. However, I do tend to make quite a few mistakes which I don't see until I read it bak.*

# Pardon my spilling

Please listen to my keybaord plight.
W£urds get muxed-ip as I try to type.
When I read bak what I typed, what dos annoy,
*Isto find that I;ve hjit the odd neightbouring  koy >
Althoufgh I'm able t0 type veryfasst,
That's when I doscover all the leters i massed.

I used to write my litters byhand.
   That's when computrs weren't arand.
I never had these proBlems then..
If oNly I cud find a pen.
   MOstly the litters E andK
Jum pp   arouond    eend ket in my "wey.
Wor doo those xktra literrs come prom#
And wy do I kep losin thm?

I find that the fhster I type,
The less sens i mike.
  Cos thekeys allseemto jummp abite
WHy, oh wy can't I getit rite?
I shoULD take moor care.
I}m like a bullin a cH9na shop – such a  full.
No, it isn~t work inas I plaNNED..

I THINK I'LL RITE IT OUT BY HOND  ..

            AND.. .  ..H A N D*!*

*Technology moves so fast nowadays and the latest thing is soon out of date. As we get older, we rely more and more on the younger generations to keep us in touch with the modern world.*

# Archie's visit

Cedric lay back in his armchair,
He'd put on a calming CD.
The music was gentle and soothing.
His wife Min was pouring the tea.

Min's biscuits were ready for dunking,
The crumpets were toasted and gold.
When Min wandered in with a tray-full,
Cedric said "What a sight to behold"

But their peaceful dream-time was soon shattered,
When there came a loud knock on the door.
Min's sister stood there with young Archie,
Their nephew of ten years, no more.

"I hope you hadn't forgotten.
We arranged this last month on the phone.
You said you'd love to have Archie
If we fancied a break on our own".

"Hello Uncle Ced and Aunt Min"
Bellowed Archie as he
ran from the car.
"I've been waiting
for ages to show you
What I can play
on my electric guitar!"

"You won't know he's here, he's no trouble"
Said his mum "and by the way,
He's brought his own toys and amusements.
There are plenty of things he can play".

There's his collection of stamps and his bugle
And a big box of games for the floor,
His Meccano, his football and sports gear,
His laptop and smartphone . . . and more.

His Lego, his schoolbooks for homework,
And his skateboard, his guitar and his drums
And his X-box and downloads of music
And his mobile for calling his chums!

(Cedric wondered: 'All *this*, for a weekend?
There's enough here to last him a year.
Entertain him? We won't even *find* him.
He'll be buried beneath all that gear').

"When I was a nipper" droned Cedric,
"We'd play with a hoop and a stick,
We were poor . . . but at least we were happy".
(He was laying it on a bit thick).

"The gifts we'd be given for Christmas?
An apple and orange alone".
Said Archie *"That's exactly what I got . . .*
*A laptop and new mobile phone!"*

With that, they both started to chuckle
By the time Min came back, they were set,
Archie was eating an apple
. . . and Cedric was 'surfing the net'.

BS/PB

*When our children were younger, we always had a lot of difficulty getting them up in the mornings. I can remember pulling them out of bed by their feet. We all found it rather amusing and they just got back in again - but they didn't manage to get back to sleep!*

*Another thing I'd do was march into their rooms, exhuberantly pull the curtains apart and I'd shout "Good morning world, what a wonderful day . . . now I'm up, gotta shout hooray!"*

*Is that annoying - or what?*

# Barbed thoughts from a home

Good morning world, what a wonderful day!
Those oppressive clouds have gone away.
The sun is shining, the sky's deep blue
But best of all it's the weekend too!

Just one or two jobs to do before
We can go for a stroll along the seashore.
I'll have to touch up and paint the ceiling,
Wallpaper that corner where the paint is peeling,

Hang curtains, mend sofa springs, dust,
Polish, wash up, iron . . . just
Wait a mo, this isn't fair.
We're stuck inside, the sun's out there!

But, as my paranoia reaches its peak,
In the distance I hear someone speak,
Followed by singing: *I'm still in bed!*
The sheets are wrapped around my head.

It's eight o'clock, that sunny day's gone
And our radio alarm has turned itself on.
Now we hear the weather forecast.
It's winter, not imagined August.

She says it's going to rain and blow,
Frosty this morning with a risk of snow.
Bad weather's due, no trip to the sea
But no more strife to worry me.

Who cares about the things to do,
For now I'll have a *clearer* view
And no concerns about the weather.
The rain can come down hell-for-leather.

The wind may rage, trees could collide,
*My sunshine's lying by my side!*

---

*In some ways my wife and I complement each other very well. In other ways we're opposites. I'm a hoarder. She's a minimalist. I'm laid back and slow. She's always on the go and finds it difficult to relax. I'm a late owl. She's an early bird. I'm usually the last to get to bed and the one who locks up at night. She's always up first in the mornings. So, if I want to surprise her with something when she gets up the following day, I can arrange it safely as I'm sorting the house out, last thing. One of my (ongoing) surprises concerned a cuddly toy called Shaun.*

# Cuddly toys and friends

Our children have both grown up and gone,
Though their cuddly toys *haven't* moved on.
      Most of them are still here.
I'll tell you all about them . . . if you'll just lend an ear.

Gromit looks down from the top of the stairs.
As for Wallace, I don't know where *he* is.
No matter from what angle you choose to view,
You'll find Gromit's looking right back at you.

No, we never had a Wallace -
      though we had Shaun the Sheep
But he's one of the few that we didn't keep.
On late evenings I'd adjust his long limbs for a while
The next day, his positions would make us all smile.

If you pressed his hand he'd sing his song
But it got quite annoying – it went on *far too long!*
So he sat in the lounge for a month or two
And then he moved on . . . to pastures new.

Then there's Winnie, Thumper , Sooty and Sweep
They are some of the ones we thought we *would* keep.
We couldn't bear to give them away.
We hoped that they'd be loved again
Maybe they will - *they might be one day!*

Most of the toys aren't on display
But one or two favourites
*still* pay their way.
Little Ted just holds a mirror
at the correct slant.
Tigger's always moving – *don't think that he can't!*

At night-time he leans 'gainst our door.
    If he doesn't, the door'll
Open too far. Next morning
    he's moved to the opposite wall.
He doesn't bounce though
    *(But when we're asleep he might have a go).*

Out in the garden, there's a little stone mole,
Which we call Morris. *He* hasn't a role.
If he was perched on a pile of earth,
    you might think he'd risen
From his underground tunnel -
    but the fact is . . . he isn'.

Also outside is Rusty the dog. He looks up at the door
And his pleading expression is hard to ignore.
He's made from old bits of metal,
    an exhaust pipe and a spring
(Which just goes to prove you can
    make toys from anything).

They've been left behind for us to look after.
In past times they've had us roaring with laughter.
We remember our children and their energy.
They were so young – and so were we!

But that was all *such* a long time ago.
Those days won't come back. They're over, I know.
Still, the toys might be useful again - they might be.
That is, if we ever have grandchildren
    *. . . then we'll see!*

*The painting above is a mural*
*which I painted for our son's nursery room.*
*We lived in a built-up area but the ideal location always*
*seems to be to live in the middle of nowhere.*

# The countryside

No swimming pool, no shopping mall,
No big prestigious concert hall,
No night club, no theatre and no cinema,
No art gallery, no stadium, etcetera, etcetera.

No building or structure of *any* importance
But do I want these things? Not me! No thanks!
Forget the town, you'll find *me* where
There's space . . . and I can breathe clean air.

No tourists or traffic jams, less crime,
No litter or graffiti and no grime,
No stress, no queues, no hassle here;
Except for tractors, roads are clear.

I go to town, then get away.
I'd rather visit . . . and not stay.
No need to ask where I would *rather* be.
It's the quiet of the countryside for me!

---

*My wife is an excellent cook and she enjoys cooking too! She started announcing "You couldn't get better in a restaurant" as she served her various concoctions.*

*It became another family saying.*

# You couldn't get better in a restaurant

I'm so glad I met my wife when I did - long ago.
Her cooking can't be bettered - I must let you know.
The food she prepares is all I'd *ever* want.
You couldn't get any better in a five star restaurant!

If you asked about my favourites, I can't think
      where I'd start.
I guess fish cakes, chicken curry, ice cream
      and treacle tart
Would be near the top if I made a list
But, then again, her steak pie is hard to resist.

She serves beans and carrots piping hot,
Which just minutes past were in the vegetable plot.
Her prowess in the kitchen - it's beyond compare.
Things grilled on toast are all I can prepare.

We've had fun through the years when she's tried
   something new.
And her attempts all bore fruit, except one . . . maybe two.
After foraging in the hedgerows, in the fields and the lanes
Her sloe gin and fruit liqueurs were quite delicious,
   in the main.

But the wines she made from elderflower
   and from elderberry
Weren't complementary to the food,
well not really, no not very.
   The worst mishap she *ever* had
   concerned her home-brewed beer.
   Thank goodness, when it happened,
   we were away . . . and nowhere near.

I recall our close escape - for on that fateful day
The beer bottles all exploded - while we were far away!
(We'd stored them all on a rack in the hall
And had to pull chunks of glass from the wall).

Then, when she thought she'd try to make bread,
At first it was solid - and as hard as lead
But, as it turned out, she had no need to frown.
For *now* her bread is the toast of the town!

To butter a crust from a just-baked loaf of bread
Is an extra special treat . . . mmm . . . 'nuff said!
I know that high on a pedestal I've set her.
But in a restaurant you wouldn't *ever* get better!

It's just food for thought . . . if I may paraphrase
And she *really is* entitled to all this praise.
She's the cream of the crop, the apple of my eye.
I'm just grateful to have a slice of the pie.

*Our son and his girlfriend have a female house-rabbit called Roo. They've recently introduced a male companion for her who they've christened Buzz . . . but they've been keeping them apart until he's been snipped.*

# The ballad of Buzz & Roo

Poor Roo was feeling rather blue,
Then one day she met someone new.
She'd been so lonely hitherto
But Buzz had an image to live up to.

Her suitor came, perchance to woo.
A ballyhoo did then ensue.
She knew what he would like to do
But hanky panky was taboo.

When he approached, she just withdrew.
Opportunities seemed all too few.
He had a different point of view.
All Buzz wanted was a screw.

When they next met he tried anew.
She feared another hullabaloo
But Buzz had met his Waterloo
And didn't want to follow through.

At last a happy home for two,
For now there's been
a big breakthrough.
Roo's had to change her
point of view
And wants to say a big 'thank you'.

*My wife is often infuriated by my ability always to see the other side in any situation. She's accepted my odd ways - like having the cold tap on the left. Every time we've moved house, we've had to swop the plumbing over - I'm sure the house where I was brought up had them that way round.*

*We seem to have suffered the experience of moving house more than most. Our friends complain that they're running out of space for us in their address books.*

*When I wrote this, my wife and I were once again stuck in that 'no-man's land' between houses - with our hearts and minds frustratingly focused on a new area whilst our bodies were held captive in our past (but still present) home.*

*Every time we moved, we hoped it would be the last time and we'd be able to stay put. We didn't really have to cope with all the problems which are detailed here in a single move but most of them have happened to us over the years.*

*Each part of the process of moving house is stressful and it doesn't necessarily end when you move in.*

# Moving story
## - an epic tale

*Prelude*

Decision made – we're moving away.
But how much can we afford to pay?
Best get the house valued – then we'll know
What we can spend and if we can go.

They say it's worth more than we could imagine.
It won't be a long time before we can cash-in.
All the estate agents seem very positive.
Now, where would we really *like* to live?

It's in the agent's window, in the paper, on the net.
We've filled the cracks and tidied so now I guess we're set
And waiting for the strangers who'll want to make a call.
We don't mind all the snooping, no of course not - not at all.

Should we walk along with them? I think we'd rather.
If we leave them alone, then they'll whisper to each other,
Or talk loudly 'bout the things they'd want to improve.
How rude!

Next the bidding process at last gets under way.
We think that it's a fair price but will anybody pay?
"It looks much bigger on the net!"
    *(They use a special lens, you know).*
"But that's a *silly* offer! We couldn't go *that* low".

We finally get an offer which we're happy to accept.
What a relief! At least our nerve we kept.
For now we've found a person who intends to buy.
Could it finally be *our* turn to fly?

*Viewings*

We cruise around our intended neighbourhood
Spying houses we can't have . . . but wish we could.
Now it's *our* turn to view - and you can bet
They won't look like they looked on the internet.

There's a noisy street right by the front door,
A pub two doors along and then what's more,
A huge industrial site behind.
Did the agent think we wouldn't mind?

The garden's so waterlogged – it's like a bog!
Dust everywhere and can you smell dog?
The church bell chimes hourly I've just been told.
No wonder these houses still haven't been sold.

All details the agents forgot to tell.
They'd say they're only trying to sell
But actually there's no reason or rhyme.
It just makes us cross and wastes valuable time.

We check the external structure and the roof
But inside we try to remain aloof.
Personal items we ought to ignore
And focus instead on wall, ceiling and floor.

How much to put all the wrong things right?
If we throw them a line do you think they'll bite?
Will they accept our offer? Yes, hooray!
Now, finally, we're on our way!

At last, this really is the one!
Now to get the survey done.
It'll need some work to make it our own
But we've finally found our ideal home.

*The move*

The buyers and sellers chain is long.
Let's hope it'll be sufficiently strong
And that no-one feels they need to back out.
Predictably, we start to doubt.

Will the chain break? Will it hold?
Is this it? Have we sold?
Now the tension is at its worst.
Tempers fray - we're fit to burst.

The solicitors deliberate,
Till they finally agree a date.
When can we hire a van - and then move in?
That's when our new life can begin.

The moving day is here – hip, hip, hooray!
And it's not raining – it's a lovely day.
The house is slowly emptying, the removal van fills up.
Another cup of tea is made: "C'mon lads, have a sup!"

We make a final check to ensure it has all gone
For, now the house is empty. It looks sad and so forlorn.
It's been our home for many a year,
We'll have to hope the new folks will be as happy here.

*Aftershock*

We've finally arrived. We're in – at last!
I'd hoped that all that tension was now over - in the past
But we hadn't thought this house would be
       in such a dreadful mess.
Would we buy the house again?
       We *still* would answer "Yes!"

It's so different without furniture. Now we can see the dust.
There's a dripping tap and broken shelves
       ... and the central heating's bust!
The wallpaper's not our taste. That'll have to be re-done
And they left us all this rubbish – but light bulbs?
       No, not a single one!

The decorative style leaves much to be desired -
Once the height of fashion but now looking rather tired.
A dark brown sink and toilet: *well, I ask you, please!*
That's so dated, so old fashioned, so 1970s.

Each room's been decorated in a different hue,
With brown and orange circles or big flowers
       in pink and blue,
Main bedroom painted black and kitchen in bright red
And who has brown toilets nowadays?
       Oh - whoops, that's just been said!

The garden also needs attention.
It's in a state – and dare I mention
Those leylandii trees? They'll have to come out!
And that'll cost us thousands – of that I have no doubt.

Have you spotted all the stuff they've left for us outside?
They said they'd take it all away –
    but no – it seems they lied!
Are we going to let it worry us? Well no, not us – we ain't.
That wallpaper can soon be covered with
    a tasteful coat of paint.

We knew it had potential – and will be right in time
But we hadn't thought it would entail such a hill to climb.
These things don't really matter - we bought it anyway:
Places with such character don't come round every day.

All that's now in the past but I'll make it very plain,
We wouldn't want to have to go through
    all that stress again.
So, please forgive my comments and every little moan,
For now we're going to change our house . . .
    so we can call it 'home'.

*In our youth we hardly ever consider it but as we get older the inevitability of death draws ever closer.*

# If you died first . . .

If you died first, what would I do?
I'd make up a list to work my way through
Of dangerous things – I'd not care about dying.
Just think of all the tasks I'd be trying.

I could learn to parachute, free fall or paraglide,
Bungee jump, climb a mountain or deep sea dive,
I'd let the Lord decide if I do or die
I'd do my best – at least I'd try.

I'd sail round the world - I'd live each day
And do whatever came my way.
I'd not be concerned if tragedy struck,
I'll go when God's ready – it's not a matter of luck.

How long we travel this road we don't know
But I'll carry on - till it's my turn to go.
I'll push myself to the limit, twenty four seven,
Till I'm with you once more
  . . . *but this time in heaven!*

# MODERN TIMES

*My first job, after leaving school, was in London at the BBC. Although it sounds very grand, the job was in fact extremely tedious. I moved from that job to another one - just as tedious, transferring files onto microfilm.*

*The one redeeming factor was that our small team was sent to most of the BBC offices around London, one after the other. I worked in a building opposite Broadcasting House, at rehearsal studios in North Acton and even at the famous Ealing Studios (which was part of the BBC then). One day, on leaving the BBC Club at lunchtime, I found myself face to face with Morecambe and Wise. "After you young sir" said Eric to me . . . TO ME!*

*My final job at the Beeb was in the Gramophone Library at Television Centre (just filing records mainly) but in my breaks and at lunchtime I'd stroll along to the Obsevation Rooms and look down to see what was going on in the studios. They might be setting or striking a set or sometimes they'd be rehearsing for a period drama or an entertainment show.*

*I might even be lucky enough to see Pan's People rehearsing for 'Top Of The Pops'!*

*It was interesting to see my fellow diners in the BBC canteen. The actors would often enter in their costumes. Once an entire Roman Legion lined up to be served.*

*My parents had a treat when they visited me at work one day and The Two Ronnies happened to be sitting at the table next to us. I could imagine my mother sharing that experience with a few friends when she got back home. I did in fact end up working at the Beeb for seven years until I went to college to study Graphic Design.*

*This poem was written much more recently but once again doing a tedious job and working in an a office with others earning much more than I was. Some of them complained about their meagre salaries. Most employees were unhappy. Nationally, there was an air of apathy and a constant fear of redundancies. Low morale was rife.*

*I took this general premise and expanded the idea. An unexpected twist presented itself as I neared the final lines, culminating in a denouement with the final word*

*. . . very satisfying!*

# The daily grind

It's hard to manage when you're poorly paid,
Doing boring work and on a low grade.
I've found it's not *what* - but *who* you know.
Small comfort, when seen from down here, far below.

Who to suck up to, who to impress?
Don't try asking me – I've made such a mess!
So much disparity 'tween me - in the mire,
Up to the whizz kids, the toffs and high flyers.

What do they find to do with their money?
Two houses? World cruises? Posh cars? It's not funny!
They earn twice, four times, ten times what I earn.
If I had what they get . . . I'd have money to burn!

Should I open my mouth or keep tightly shut?
No, I'll just have to accept that I'm stuck in a rut.
With redundancies and job losses rife,
It's no use complaining - it's not fair but that's life.

When I tell of my troubles, they think it's a joke
But I've still got my health and I'm not a bad bloke.
I have got a job - I ought not to be sour.
I know, I'll surprise someone now
   . . . with my buttonhole flower.

Where are we next? A different site? Or a new town?
Anyway, it's time for the baggy pants
   and painted frown.

Of course - not *everyone* can be a clown!

---

*Both of our children are adopted. They've left home now and set up their own homes. Our son is from Crewe and our daughter was born in Romania. We'd already adopted our son in this country and it was proving difficult to adopt another child. In 1990 we watched a television programme about Romanian orphanages. It changed our lives.*

*We were horrified to see neglected Romanian children in filthy conditions living in orphanages which looked more like prisons. Their obvious distress was heart rending.*

*President Ceausescu had a policy of encouraging his people to produce at least five children. Many of the parents weren't able to support them and the orphanages were, consequently, full. His firm grip on the country ended with a revolution which flared up at the end of 1989 followed by another smaller revolution in June 1990. When Ceausescu was finally overthrown, prospective adoptive parents from all over the world turned to Romania and for a few years there was an open door to that country.*

*When the programme had finished, we both started wondering whether it would be possible to adopt a child ourselves and after a few months that's exactly what we did. Our daughter was three when we brought her to England. She looks and sounds English and that's what she is. It got me wondering how we identify a person as belonging to a particular country.*

*So-called British or English sportsmen and women sometimes have very foreign sounding names and some speak English with a very pronounced accent. They could qualify to play for our country if their parents or even their grandparents were born here.*

# What makes us English ?

What makes us English? It's hard to tell.
With so many cultures, what makes us gel?
We once had an empire which stretched far and near.
Then we gave them their freedom,
        now they're all coming here.

What of invasions? We've had quite a few,
But they've all left us something, to give them their due.
Vikings from Denmark, Romans from Rome,
Normans from France, they've all called this home.

Looking back further, what became of the Celts?
They all headed west – now they're Irish or Welsh.
Even Anglo Saxons come from Saxony
And isn't that in Germany?

And how about food? What's our national dish?
Is it curry or pizza? Is it still chips and fish?
What makes us English? It's not very clear.
What's our national tipple? It used to be beer.

In past times 'twas Mead. It then became Ale:
Dark Brown in Newcastle, in East Anglia Pale.
The Irish drink Guinness, Scots a wee dram.
The Danish like lager, the French have their vin.

Posh people sip Pimm's or perhaps Gin and Tonic
But most drinks will suffice - if they're alcoholic.
There's Tequila and Ouzo and Sherry and Port
Cider and Vermouth - there are long drinks and short.

Choosing something that's English – now what could it be?
Should we settle perhaps for a big mug of tea?
What makes us English? What's our national sport?
All those foreigners play the ones that we've taught.

To throw an oblong ball backwards,
      how to bowl at a wicket,
Serve a ball with a racquet or with a mallet hit it.
To play snooker and darts or to head at a goal,
How to cheat with your hand if you're not very tall
      *(that's you Maradona)*

They don't play the game in the way that they should
But they're better than us; they've all got too good.
They try too hard, that's not how it's done.
They play to win, it's just meant to be fun!

When I greet someone nowadays, what do I say?
"Why-aye Pet, Wazzup, Ow-do, Have a nice day?"
Or should I speak 'modern', I'm not sure if I could:
"Hello, how-ya doin?" "Hi, thank you, I'm good."

Who runs our companies? Who owns our banks?
Even our language has been abused by the Yanks.
We don't eat French fries or put jelly on bread
And it's not sidewalk or highway - *use **our** words instead!*

What of our heritage – our Queens and our Kings?
After verse one of our anthem, hardly anyone sings.
Nothing's straight forward. I'm filled with confusion.
Is the notion we're English merely illusion?

So many religions. To which God do we pray?
But would I live elsewhere? The answer's "No way!"
What makes us English? I'm *still* not too clear.
Well let's say *we are*
    . . . just as long as we *live* here.

*My parents always told me how I should behave in different circumstances - at the dinner table, on a bus or just walking on the pavement (where you should walk on the outside so that your companion won't get splashed).*

*The chief emphasis was that you should always put the other person first and yourself last. Sadly, those good manners are now largely forgotten.*

# Put the other person first

The trouble with the world today
Is the rise of self-importance and what we say.
Celebrities abound, now anyone's a star.
But highlighting one's self has gone too far.

Take a back seat, learn to give,
Both grammatically and in the way you live.
Put yourself last. That's the key
And live a life more care-fully.

I was taught to say "my friend and I".
Today it's "me and my friend".
Sadly it's just a courtesy
That now we *don't* extend.

All troubles stem from this subtle change.
It determines how we think.
You may scoff and shake your head.
Can you deny that there's a link?

Let's revive that spirit of the past.
Put the other person first and *your self* last.
It's time to let that other person take the lead.
A simple change of attitude is really all we need!

With neighbour, colleague, husband, wife,
In your speech . . . and accordingly in life,
Put the *other* person first – not you.
That's what we *all* should strive to do.

---

*Jack and Jill didn't just fall over. They often fell out too!*
*This is a short take on what might have happened*
*after they fell down the hill.*

# Jack and Jill

Jack and Jill went for a walk.
On their way they had a talk.
The talk soon turned into a row.
Jack called Jill a silly cow.
She ran away
    . . . Jack's single now!

---

*The following poem is a comment on commercialism*
*and that the real meaning of Christmas is now just*
*an afterthought.*

# Have you been good?

Secret Santa, office parties,
Tinsel on computer screens,
Christmas cake and tins of biscuits,
Over-eating, feeling green.

Jostling with bad tempered shoppers,
Buying gifts to be refunded.
Aching backs and fingers stinging,
Over heating, turning red.

Stocking up with boxes
Full of spirits, beer and wine.
Is this the *best* way to ensure
That we'll be having a good time?

Cards to long forgotten friends
And children asked "Have you been good?"
Doorstep, tone deaf carol singers -
"I'm not going to the door. - I think you should!"

Long distance trips through blizzards,
Snow, fog, ice and rain.
Family members meeting up,
Then falling out again.

Party games, torn paper hats,
Turkey, pud, mince pies,
The Sound Of Music, The Great Escape,
The Queen, Morecambe and Wise.

Useless gifts and jokes from crackers,
Fudge, sweets, dates and figs.
Lying in a stupor,
Having eaten just like pigs.

Then later, thank-you letters for unwanted presents,
Washing up and hoovering.
Oh - and wasn't there a baby
Born to be our saviour
       . . . and our King ?

---

*When you have anyone to stay, it's always best to show an interest in whatever they're keen on. So it was that Cedric decided to have a game of football - but it was useless telling Minnie that it's just a game . . .*

# Min's reign stops play

There's a triumphal Arch over Wembley,
Where footballers all yearn to play.
That's why Min's nephew was 'Arch-ie',
(He was born on a Cup Final day).

When he came to stay they were anxious
To keep the young lad entertained.
They agreed to a game in the garden,
After lunch if it hadn't just rained.

Cedric had thought of absconding
But when he'd had one of his pills
He thought he'd impress his young nephew,
Demonstrating his old football skills.

"You can play in the garden" said Minnie
"But don't make a mess of the lawn,
And don't you go near my tomatoes
Or you'll wish that you'd never been born."

So Cedric waited out on the patio
With a football and ready to play.
Archie was still in his bedroom,
Selecting his kit for the day.

He came out in a black and white outfit,
Like a humbug straight out of the box,
But Cedric was certain he'd top that,
With his trousers tucked
into his socks.

Now Archie's away-kit was stripey,
He'd worked out that really made sense,
He thought the old boy
wouldn't see him,
As his shirt would
blend-in with the fence.

But Cedric was wise
to his game-plan,
And didn't give Archie the ball.
He called it 'retaining possession',
And played on his own by the wall.

"I was fast as a youngster" said Cedric
"I'd leave an opponent for dead
And cross the ball over to Lofty,
Who'd bounce the ball in, off his head".

Min had sat down in her deckchair,
She'd appointed herself referee.
She'd a whistle, a pen and a notebook
And red cards like she'd seen on TV.

She blew the whistle for kick-off,
Then blew it again to make sure -
The two boys were having a beano,
And no-one remembered the score.

Now Min loved the sound of that whistle,
But she blew it too often, for fun.
First she sent-off her Cedric for 'diving'
When slipping was all that he'd done.

She also red-carded young Archie
For arguing and 'persistent foul play'
"There's too much of this sort of thing happening"
She said. "You're the second I've sent off today".

Though how the game's played is what matters,
Not caring to lose or to win,
The stalemate was suddenly shattered
With a wild pitch invasion by Min.

The game between Cedric and Archie
Had ended in complete disarray
She'd sent off both of the players
And blew early to end
the day's play.

"Calm down, dear"
said Cedric to Minnie,
"You're forgetting it's only a game".
But her answer was rude and bad tempered,
Then she whistled . . . and booked him again!

Our Cedric was losing his patience,
He thought Min's decisions unfair
He even tried tearing his hair out . . .
But there wasn't enough left to tear.

Their neighbour said "Oy, keep the noise down".
He was in a bad mood, Min could tell
But our Minnie was having no nonsense . . .
She sent off the neighbour as well.

Min had enjoyed all this action -
The kicking and shouting and tears,
And the fighting and biting and brawling,
She'd not had as much fun for years.

But Cedric was secretly worried.
Was this the nice lass that he'd wed?
He'd not seen this dark side of Minnie.
Had authority gone to her head?

She goose stepped her way round the garden,
Just stopping to caution the cat,
She sent off the budgie for whistling,
"It's just me who's allowed to do that".

Min's sights were set higher than football,
She'd much more important things planned,
She marched her way down to the High Street,
Intent on invading Poundland.

The butcher was given a roasting,
The girl in the café was grilled
The man in the bread shop was toasted,
In Iceland the outlook was chilled.

The man in the fish shop got battered,
Round here they still speak of the crime,
Min explained the attack didn't matter,
After all it was *injury time.*

At last she came back to her senses:
"What on earth has been happening to me?
I've become a right little dictator,
Since I started to play referee".

Min threw her red cards in a puddle,
She vowed she'd play football no more.
She went home and gave Cedric a cuddle.
They decided they'd call it a draw.

Young Archie'd enjoyed the weekend.
He really had been entertained.
He just couldn't wait for half-term time,
To come back and do it again!

BS/PB

---

*Bucket lists are all the rage today. These are lists of things to do before you die (ie. kick the bucket). They're usually adventurous and seemingly unobtainable things.
Having such a list will surely put a lot of pressure on you to complete it.*

# A hole in my bucket list

There's a hole in my bucket list. Can you see it dear reader?
My bucket is empty - I don't *know* what to do.
I'll never complete all those wondrous adventures.
All the tasks I imagined have all fallen through.

I won't climb a mountain, appear in a movie
Travel the world, or learn how to ski,
Run in a marathon, see the Aurora Borealis,
Climb the Empire State Building, swim in the Dead Sea.

From now on I'm going to be more realistic.
That list was outrageous. I'm feeling letdown.
So I'll stand in my garden and see my *own* sunrise.
I'll climb a small hill, I'll jog into town.

Why did I come up with such absurd aspirations?
That's the *end* of my lists. I'll do things that *aren't* planned.
I'll go to the seaside, I'll gaze into rock pools.
I'll buy a *new* bucket *and fill it with sand!*

---

*It seems that every other nation has become so protective of its own language - not surprising really when English is so dominant.*

*What they're concerned about is losing their heritage.*

# Everyone speaks English now

*Everyone* knows English in international events.
So why bother to relay it all again - *in French?*
Just use the dominant language of the planet.
Speak in English - *every* nation understands it.

And why do all instructions
	(if you've purchased something new)
Take up to seven pages when just one would *surely* do?
Those words are just gobbledegook –
	they can't be comprehended.
If they wrote it all in English, no-one *should* be offended.

*England,* the cradle of culture,
	with the best language to speak.
The only pure language - I'll not be oblique.
Foreigners should all speak English
	as we do in good old Blighty.
If we use our common parlance – why be so hoity-toity?

But as tempus fugit I just think 'wait a mo'.
Perhaps my attitude should not be so gung-ho!
I guess it's true that pride precedes a fall
And maybe English words aren't English after all.

A propos, I see an itsy-bitsy glitch in my argument
	. . . a faux pas
And now I feel like a schmuck.
	Oh well, c'est la vie, que sera sera.

Time to vamoose . . . toodle-oo
	. . . that's all for now.
After that smorgasbord of spiel,
I guess I'd better just say
	. . . "ciao".

*One day, some-one I was working with challenged me to write a poem about a plastic bag which she'd noticed outside. It got me thinking about all the rubbish that's gathered around us which we've just come to accept as normal.*

# Plastic bag

Plastic bag blowing in the wind,
Fag ends, food packed in cardboard . . . or tinned.
All this rubbish should be binned.

At lunchtime I watch people throw things away.
Don't they know there'll be a price to pay.
That's what the TV experts say.

Standards aren't what they were in days of yore.
Now, no-one cleans the pavement by their own front door.
*People just don't care anymore.*

*St. Francis of Assisi is reputed to have said 'Preach the Gospel at all times and if necessary use words'. It's not clear if he actually said these words but he certainly approved of the meaning. Christians should let their attitudes and their deeds speak for themselves but we all fail from time to time.*

*The media seem to relish highlighting those who let the side down. Sadly it's noticeable that Christians in television programmes are invariably portrayed in a bad light.*

# Why is it always the Vicar?

When I'm watching a TV thriller I've come to realise
That it's obvious who's responsible
       for the victim's untimely demise.
If there's a clergyman in the cast list,
       it always turns out the same.
So, why is it always the vicar who gets to take the blame?

If there's a blackmailer in the story,
       you can guess who it's likely to be.
A philanderer, a pimp or a murderer –
       the answer's clear to see.
It's inevitable that a man of the cloth
       will be made to fit the bill.
Or, at the least, he'll be the one who's been caught
       with his hand in the till.

In Bergerac, Lovejoy, Hetty Wainthrop and Morse
The vicar's a bad'un - you'll have noticed of course.
In Midsomer, Northumberland, Dorset and Denton,
In Glasgow and London – the list just goes on.

It could be a Curate or Bishop, no-one is *ever* left out.
A Christian will be the bad apple - there's never any doubt.
For every clerical part, it's apparently seen as fair game.
But not all the clergy are like that.
       The writers give them a bad name.

Why is it always the Vicar who turns out
       to be the bad guy?
It must be the writers' decision –
       I'd really like to know why.

# Old woman

There was an old woman - she had a cold . . . *a-tish-ooo!*
"It's not that" she wheezed "I reckon it's flu!"
Her nose streamed and streamed,
          no matter *how* much she blew,
Her fingers were wrinkled, her throat full of glue.

So she rubbed her extremities
          with some warmed-up fish stew.
She had so many chilblains. What was she to do?
Now they're gone, so's her cold -
          but some symptoms are new.
She's *now* plagued by cats and they mew, how they mew!

So fish scales can treat chilblains - that's amazing!
          Who knew?
Of course, it's made up . . . *but could it be true?*

---

*As young children, my friend and I used to play in a back street outside an old factory building with railway lines embedded into the road surface. I can remember steam locomotives shunting trucks into the other end of the street. That was before Health and Safety regulations strangled our collective independence.*

*Another friend and I used to row up and down the river in his wooden rowing boat. We enjoyed climbing and running along a nearby weir. Although they loved us, our parents weren't unduly worried about where we played.*

# Children today

Today's parents seem
    to have lost the knack
Of how to look after their little brat.
It's a dangerous world,
    a child needs to prepare.
Cotton wool wrapping's not the best way to care.
Children should walk to school on their own.
Let them play in the park - allow them to roam!

Back in the fifties, we kicked a football.
We rode on our bikes. We flicked cards 'gainst a wall.
Just yards away, steam trains shunted trucks,
No fence between us, no signs and no fuss.
We had the sense to keep out of the way
And oh how I long for that now distant day.

Today's safety conscious society's to blame.
Children learn from mistakes that they won't make again.
We used to climb apple trees. We got wet in the rain.
We managed to get on and off moving trains.
We rowed on a river, we even played on a weir
With dangerous currents . . . and look, I'm still here!

*Innovations happen so fast nowadays. We only just get used to the latest gadget when it's superseded. Some of us strive to keep up with these technological changes. I don't! I still play LPs occasionally and have hung on to a collection of video tapes. People in Africa were using CDs before I managed to catch up. I do play CDs now but I still prefer using cassette tapes. My mobile phone is a very simple version. I don't access the internet with it and I can't be bothered to text.*

*I think it might have the facility to take photographs but I've got a camera for that job. I do sit at a computer almost every day and happily surf the net but I'm distrustful of internet banking. As for 'the hole in the wall' . . .*

# ATMs

I leaned against the window pane
And sighed as I peered at the rain.
A lot to do - I'd have to dash
*Then I discovered I'd got no cash!*

I checked my pockets - my heart sank.
It would take a while to get to the bank!
By the time I arrived, I was clearly wet through.
Then I made a decision I'd later rue.

A queue! I looked down anxiously.
T'was time to embrace the 21st century
And try to use the ATM.
(I'd never used one – not till then!)

If others could manage, then I could too!
It couldn't be that hard to do.
I thought it would be a piece of cake,
Then it dished out the cash. *"Oh, for goodness sake!"*

*It dished out a hundred. I wanted ten!*
So I queued and put it back again
Well £90 of it. *"I'm in a hurry – can't you see?"*
*Stupid blasted technology!*

Then to get some chocolates too.
Surprise, surprise, another queue.
I've not used those things before:
*I shall not use them anymore!*

56

*I worked at a Garden centre for a few years as an outside assistant doing all sorts of jobs - advising and assisting customers, re-stocking, general weeding, collecting trolleys, and occasionally compiling outdoor floral displays.*

*Prior to that I'd spent a couple of very tiring months at a Nursery, mainly digging up and carrying trees for 'bare rooted' sales. That wasn't suitable work for older folk but the Garden Centre welcomed the expertise and life experience of their more mature staff.*

# At the Garden Centre

In the spring, the Fitzwilliams had felt the need
To earn a few extra bob.
Then, at their local Garden Centre,
They were offered part-time jobs.

Cedric had said
he preferred the fresh air
And was put in the
car park outside,
Collecting the trolleys
and directing the cars.
He managed it all in his stride.

He gathered up the trolleys in a long line.
He picked up the litter. He kept it all clean.
He did his job well. He managed just fine.
He made it the tidiest it *ever* had been.

Meanwhile a delivery of shrubs had been made
And Min had been asked to assist.
She had to confirm how many were there
And ensure they all matched with her list.

There were thirty Gardenia Jasminoides
And thirty Abeliophyllum distichums.
She was told to learn all about them,
Including the Latin translations.

She discovered the Abeliophyllum
Was a white flowering kind of Forsythia
But, as she wheeled them through a side door,
She was suddenly stopped by a customer.

The trouble all started when he asked
If she'd pass down a bottle of bleach.
He needed to clean his stone path
But the bottle was just out of reach.

With her Zimmer frame used as a ladder,
She climbed up to reach the top shelf.
Min wouldn't ask for assistance,
She thought she could manage herself.

But suddenly she lost her balance.
All the shelves began to give way
With a deafening crack and a twang and a crash,
She fell into a floral display.

All the bottles and packs were sent flying
Then each hit the ground with a thud!
And the gathering crowd was engulfed
In a cloud of fish, bone and blood.

But Min was extremely fortunate -
She hadn't been injured at all.
She'd landed on her Abeliophyllum
And the shrubs had cushioned her fall.

Some sharp, thorny bushes fell on top of the pile,
Pyrocantha, Crataegus and the like
But her Zimmer frame landed above her,
To shield her from all the sharp spikes.

Her customer spied a hand with a bottle
Protruding from amid the mêlée.
He bent down and gratefully took it,
Turned about and then went off to pay.

The manager appeared in a rage
And he didn't half give her what-for.
He wouldn't risk this sort of thing any more
So Min was dismissed . . . to make sure.

After Minnie's unfortunate dismissal,
Cedric stayed on in the store.
And life at the Garden Centre
Seemed to carry on much as before.

A disgruntled Min kept her head down
And month after month drifted by.
Then one day a recruitment poster appeared
And Min thought that she would apply.

The manager had long since departed
And the new man was happy to talk.
An appointment was thereby arranged -
For the next day at seven o'clock.

He asked her to tell him the difference
'Twixt a Pergola and a Pelargonium.
Min's Latin knowledge was shaky
But she knew the answer to that one.

Her interview went very well
And they struck up a healthy rapport.
He thought she deserved a fresh chance,
So Minnie was welcomed once more.

Cedric took her off to the nursery,
Where a field was reserved for cut flowers.
They were told to plant masses of bulbs.
It would probably take them five hours.

They thought that would keep Minnie busy.
What harm could she possibly do?
But Minnie had thought of a scheme
And the two of them quickly set to.

She used her Zimmer frame as a 'dibber'
And they were able to achieve so much more.
For instead of making one hole at a time,
A shrewd Minnie was fashioning four.

Cedric walked closely beside her.
He threw a bulb into
each of the holes.
As Min shuffled,
she filled up the holes again
And so each of them stuck
to their role.

As a result of that little routine,
They'd finished in less than two hours,
Then they found themselves back in the car park
Gathering trolleys and directing the cars.

Min thought she'd help Mr Trubshaw,
Loading purchases into his car.
But she couldn't retrieve the trolley
When it got stuck on his tow-bar.

Mr Trubshaw sat in the drivers seat
While she loaded plants in the boot.
Min waived to attract his attention.
He just thought 'twas a friendly 'salute'.

She placed her Zimmer frame onto the trolley
And tried pulling the darned thing free.
Then she slammed the boot lid in frustration
And looked around anxiously.

As he turned up the radio volume,
She bellowed "Just wait a mo!"
But he wasn't paying attention to her
And he thought she'd said "Off you go".

Mr Trubshaw then started his car
But as the trolley passed by, she fell in.
He carefully drove onto the main road
And set off with Minnie behind him.

The car sped off into the distance
As Cedric looked on from afar.
Then he waved down another driver
Shouting "Please, can you follow that car?"

Mr Trubshaw thought his car was quite sluggish.
He'd not heard Min's calls of distress.
He *had* noticed a change with the steering
But continued on his way nonetheless.

Cedric's driver said "My name is Derek
We'll soon catch them up, don't you worry.
But they've already got a long way ahead
So I reckon that we'll have to hurry."

Derek's car had been left far behind,
Whilst Mr Trubshaw drove on unaware.
Min wondered what else she could do,
Then she waved her Zimmer frame in the air.

Mr Trubshaw drove on ever faster
But then hit a bump in the road.
That sudden jolt broke the deadlock
And, at last, it released his rear load.

As they'd just reached the brow of a steep hill,
The trolley wasn't inclined to remain.
It started to travel in the opposite direction
And soon picked up speed once again.

Derek's car was just climbing the hill
When they saw it descending their way.
As they watched it hurtling towards them,
It started to swerve and to sway.

Minnie was trying to steer it.
Sparks flew as it slid side to side.
Cedric raised his arms in stark horror
But Min was *enjoying* the ride!

Then she spied a car coming towards her.
She'd have to do something more drastic.
So she lent out whilst holding the Zimmer.
Her next movements were gloriously gymnastic.

Her frame landed firmly on the side of the road
And Min had made sure to hold on.
She performed a spectacular cartwheel
To mark an impressive
denouement.

The trolley
shot into some trees
But Min landed back on her feet.
She lifted her arms, gave a cheer,
And collapsed in a haphazard heap.

Then Cedric rushed to her side.
She looked up and wimpered "Whoopee".
But Cedric had made a decision
And he was hopeful that she would agree.

He held her in his arms and he whispered
"The Garden Centre's not right for us.
With loose shelves and thorns and trolleys and stuff,
*It's too blinkin' dangerous!"*

*This Valentine message is written in praise of a sporting all-rounder, a superwoman of sport.*

# A sporting Valentine

I've admired you from long distance,
></br>from the very start,
You're a star performer,
></br>you're a class apart.
I'm in the crowd to cheer you
></br>when you're the winner of a race.
I'm the one who shouts encouragement -
></br>each time you serve an ace.

I long to be your cricket bat
></br>when you practice in the nets.
How I wish that you would hug me
></br>like you grip your tennis racket.
I'd be your sparring partner
></br>when you're boxing in the ring.
If I could get that close to you,
></br>I'd do most anything.

If you're looking for a partner,
></br>I hope *I'm* who you'll pick.
I don't want to be the ball
></br>that you bat or shove or kick.
I don't wish to be a javelin
></br>and then be thrown away.
I want to spend my life with you,
></br>forever and a day.

You are the winner's trophy,
> in rugby you're the try,
In snooker a 147 break,
> in darts you're the bullseye,
You're the winning goal
> in the top of the net,
You're the L, O, V and E
> in my sporting alphabet.

You know that I look up to you,
> though you don't quite reach my height,
You're the undefeated champion,
> the rest are out of sight.
You've got me on the ropes,
> so just give me a sign!
I would be so excited
> if you were my Valentine.

You'll find me in the crowd,
> no matter what the sport.
Can you guess who's written this?
> Now, the ball is in *your* court.
Have you worked out, can you imagine,
> can you deduce who I am yet?
Have you an idea? Can you surmise?
> Just think, what's your best bet?

Now, as the whistle is raised
> to blow full time,
I fear I'm running out of rhyme,
So say you'll be my Valentine,
You know I'm yours
> - will you be mine?

# Goldilocks

Goldilocks slept in the nude,
I guess you'll think that's rather rude
But no-one knew . . . until the night
The fire alarm went off. In her fright,
She grabbed a sheet
And ran out starkers to the street.

She'd left the house in such a rush,
      in her panic, that's all she could find
And, though she was covered at the front,
      she had a bear behind
. . . *well three, actually!*

*One Sunday morning at church, I noticed a lady standing in the aisle and looking lost. I gestured to her that there was space for her in our pew. At this she retreated and then re-appeared to usher a large gentleman into the now vacant spot. He had a strong odour of alcohol and was soon asleep and balancing on my shoulder. As it turned out, he was a 'gentle giant' but I might have thought twice about offering him the space next to me.*

*A thought occurred to me that, as Christians, while we might try to do 'the right thing', God is full of surprises. He has his own agenda.*

*He will always challenge us to think 'outside the box'.*

*A couple of nights later - it was in fact in the early hours -
I woke up from a bad dream and couldn't get back to sleep.
The wording which forms a major part of this poem
came to me then.*

# You know my name

I love you Lord, I know you love me too
Before my time, *my* life you knew.
So guide me with an open hand
And I will be as you have planned.

When I think I've got it all just right
Make me aware that I just *might*
Have got it wrong; fill me anew,
And tell me what I ought to do.

If you're with me I know I can be sure
When troubles come I *will* endure.
I know you'll help me see them through.
I praise your name, I worship you.

I thank you that you bled and died for me
When you were just the one of three.
I know that you forgave my sin.
I spread *my* arms to let you in.

I know for now and then for evermore
To please you is what I live for.
Throughout eternity the same,
I thank you that *you* know my name.

*Sudbury in Suffolk is my home town, although I haven't lived there since I left home at the age of seventeen. The river which runs through Sudbury is the Stour (pronounced stoo-er). It's a beautiful river - in fact much of the Stour valley is designated as an 'Area of Outstanding Natural Beauty'.*

*Two influential eighteenth century artists hail from the Stour valley. Thomas Gainsborough was born and brought up in Sudbury. John Constable was born in East Bergholt - a village a few miles to the east.*

*Both artists painted landscapes on and around the river, the most notable being Constable's paintings a little further downstream of The Hay Wain and Flatford Mill.*

*I'm especially cross with anyone who pronounces the name of the river incorrectly. Unfortunately, that's how the more recent London overspill incomers tend to say it. I always shout at the television in disgust anytime it's referred to as such.*

# The River Stour

Beware, before you make a sound,
Lest you stand on dodgy ground.
It rhymes with truer – not with tower.
Pronounce it stoo-er – it's *not* the stow-er.

I grew up near the river banks
And if you want to gain my thanks,
In good will and as a token,
Please say it as it *should* be spoken.

The indigenous dwellers say it right.
Newcomers *won't* be contrite.
And though I've now moved far away,
I'm still *incensed* with what they say.

Please say it right - try to make sure.
Just don't imagine that you're
Eating something that tastes sour.
Say with a smile, not with a glower.

We all know words which aren't too clear.
When you're not sure, just use your ear.
And listen to what the locals say,
Then copy them – say it *their* way!

TV presenters don't seem to try
To make an effort and comply:
Those they talk to say it true.
It's really not so hard to do.

Make an ooooh sound – not an ow,
I hope you'll say it *their* way now.
Before you speak, please,
please make sure.
*Newer . . . truer . . . pure*
*. . . Stour!*

# Common sense

It's best *never* to credit folk with having common sense.
You'll only be frustrated - 'cos some can be quite dense.
Mental capacity isn't relevant - well, not in this respect
For common sense has no regard for higher intellect.

Of dangers in the home, we *all* should be aware
Of ladders, tools and gadgets, pots and pans . . .
        and steps and stairs.
We all should be receptive to our *own* welfare
But sense is far from common - it's comparatively rare.

On the roads, the ablest drivers can still surprise us all
When sadly they don't appreciate the safer protocols.
They'll cut corners, double park, go too fast, tailgate
Just use some common sense - that's what I advocate!

Our leaders are short sighted. They avoid the hard decisions.
They don't worry 'bout the environment.
        They have no future vision.
But we're all to blame - and we're running out of time.
We're in a mess. It makes no sense. When will we draw a line?

We don't hold dear the wider world which God left in our care.
The evidence surrounds us - neglect is everywhere.
We should stop using fossil fuels - its time to look ahead.
Why can't we just rely on the sun and wind instead?

In the summer it's too hot - in the winter it's too wet.
Our sense should be refined but we *ignore* the threat.
With imminent global warming or a possible deep freeze,
Let's acknowledge all the warning signs

        *. . . and don't cut down the trees!*

# THE PLACE TO BE

*My wife and I were involved in The York Mystery Plays in 2012, portraying various scenes from the Bible. They're revived every few years and involve a large cast of local residents - many of whom have no experience of theatre work. It's a big community project.*

*This scene depicts a stand-off between Jesus and the devil, surrounded by swirling angels.*

*A huge auditorium was set up in the Museum Gardens and
the ruined abbey walls acted as an impressive backdrop.
I especially remember Noah and the flood with hordes
of cast members raising their umbrellas to portray the
raging waves and also a wide trapdoor in the centre of the
stage with red smoke billowing from below and a crowd of
dejected people walking down the steps to 'hell'.*

# It's a mystery

Alpha and Omega, from beginning to the end.
The word made flesh, a life 'mongst us -
> but destined to ascend.
Stories from the Bible - tales of truths and lies,
Of good and evil, heaven and hell -
> and a long lost paradise.

The world below, the world above -
A story of eternal love.

Adam and Eve's existence in the unbridled joy of Eden,
Then in desperation when that forbidden fruit was eaten.
The ark which Noah had to build to escape the devastation,
Which granted a new beginning
> through resulting re-creation.

The stand-off 'twixt the Magi and the despotic
> King of decadence,
Then the sudden brutal slaughter of unprotected innocents.

Miracles performed, an unlikely ministry begun
And all by one who dared to claim to be our Father's son.
How a triumphant entry to the city
> and the crowd's loud cheering
Just days later turned to bitterness,
> hate, loathing, scorn and jeering.

Betrayal and arrest, conviction and crucifixion,
Death on a cross - then life again
> but only through absolution.

What's the point? Why the effort? Why the mystery?
It's the name of many plays handed down
> throughout our history.
Despite the shambolic mess we're in
> since Adam's fateful fall,
It's a timely reminder that Jesus lives . . .

*and died to save us all.*

*Music brings colour into our lives - how dull would life be without it? Certain music has the power to transport us to another time and place.*

# Go Min go!

Cedric had taken Min shopping.
His job was to carry it all.
He was starting to get a bit grumpy
But Minnie was having a ball.

But why on earth wasn't she tiring?
His legs and his feet were quite sore.
Then he realised (when he glanced at her zimmer)
That she had an extra four!

"I say Min, I'm craving a coffee"
Said Cedric. He needed a break.
They'd spent all the morning in clothes shops.
It was time for a rest - and some cake.

So they searched for a suitable café
And found one called 'Frothy Flynn'.
Cedric went to the counter and ordered,
Then sat down on a sofa with Min.

Now 'Frothy Flynn' thought himself clever -
He'd noticed them open the door,
So he played a CD on the jukebox
In the hope that they'd stay and spend more.

The next track caught their attention.
It took them back to their very first date.
'Twas one they remembered
they'd danced to,
Back in 1958.

The song had a special
meaning for them
And Min wouldn't
give up this chance.
"C'mon Cedric,
this one is our tune.
Remember when
we used to dance?"

"See you later, alligator"
she whispered in his ear,
"In a while crocodile" he sighed
"Remember my dear
We're not quite as agile as we used to be".
Min said "Humbug, c'mon and just follow me".

Their jiving grew ever more frantic,
As they boogied along with the beat.
"I'm gone, real gone" blurted Minnie
"I just can't keep up with my feet".

But then Cedric knocked over some people
(Who had tried to keep out of his way)
Then fell into the arms of a waitress
And knocked all the food off her tray.

Glasses and crockery went flying,
Doughnuts rolled out through the door.
There was froth down all of the windows,
Cappuccinos splashed over the floor.

The floor had become very slippery,
Folk were sliding around on their knees.
'Frothy Flynn' thought they were all dancing,
So he stayed where he was, looking pleased.

When all the commotion was over
And the jiving had finally stopped,
Cedric and Min were exhausted.
They'd bopped until they'd dropped.

They collapsed in a heap on the sofa
And their joints were now starting to ache.
'Frothy Flynn' had really enjoyed it
And he served them with extra cake.

He said "Please do a demonstration
For the pensioners next week".
The pair declined politely,
Though they found it hard to speak.

"I think we'll take things easy,
Stay at home and just relax".
Then they called in at the chemist's,
To buy ointments for their backs.

The lesson of this story
Is to keep things 'caffeine-free'.
If you're thirsty
when out shopping
... don't have coffee,
stick to tea.

BS/PB

*As a young man, my father had been a very enthusiastic rower and had won loads of cups and trophies as a member of the Stour Boat Club (remember to pronounce it 'stoo-er'). Although I was always interested in rowing, I never took it up seriously.*

*My main interest as a young teenager was making 8mm 'Cine' (Movie) films. This was in the days before video cameras had been invented. I shared the interest with one of my friends. We'd both been inspired by a film we'd seen in the cinema called 'The Great Race' (starring Tony Curtis and Jack Lemmon) and decided to make our own version - but as a boat race. There was no sound, except for a musical soundtrack which we played on a cassette recorder - so it wasn't possible to synchronise the sound all that accurately.*

*My chief recollection of the filming process was of the passsionate arguments which my friend and I had at various locations along the river because we both wanted to be the director. Although the end result was surprisingly acceptable, I tended to work on films on my own after that.*

*We recently stayed with him and his wife for a few days and spent one glorious day reminiscing on the river.*

*This poem says it all !*

# A day on the river

Blue sky, soft breeze - *ideal* rowing weather.
The four of us decide that we'll all go together.
But parental duties mean that one of us can't come,
So we continue anyway ... but as a threesome.

My other half will operate the rudder - she's unsure
　　　　but nonetheless
We'll both be facing backwards so she must chart
　　　　our progress.
She has the most important job - to steer.
For only she can guarantee
　　　　our way is clear.

We climb aboard and push the boat out -
> *and we're underway!*

The sun glints on the water - it's a perfect day.
Our boat is gently rocking side to side,
As onward now we glide.

We marvel at the wildlife show,
The chirping sparrows call to us below.
Whilst fish wait for their chance and then dance past
And swans and ducks ask to be added to the cast.

The gentle trickle as our bow cuts through,
A sombre frame of mind seems to imbue.
An ongoing splash from oars adds to the sound.
What paradise we've found!

The sweet singing of small birds, a rustling in the trees,
The gentle movement of the water lilies - and the reeds.
There's hardly any weed getting tangled with the oars
So rowing is much easier of course.

Yet at times we find we're making heavy weather.
We employ a steady rhythm and try to work together.
Then we break into a spurt and sense the thrill
    of moving fast.
And watch the glorious countryside surge past.

The scene before us gradually recedes
As stroke by stroke we pick up speed.
For now we've moved into third gear.
Expanding ripples spread out to the rear.

Our arms stretch forward till we dip our oars,
Then pull back sharply - to enforce
The boat to sprint ahead
And now an imaginary race has started.

Our phantom adversaries pull away
We'll not be beaten - *not today!*
Edging closer, we're slowly gaining, then we're level.
We're an inch or two ahead, then several.

We must increase our speed
But with *one* stroke *they're* in the lead.
Back and forth, then us, then them
And then it's us again.

We have to stop. We're both exhausted
>*but we've won the race!*

We limp forward, now at a much slower pace.
Blades splash as oars scarce rise and fall.
The river's harmonies enthral.

On either shore we stare in awe
At damsel and dragonflies galore.
The melodic singing of the birds which sweetly call
All herald the closing stages of our delightful haul.

Then, on rounding the next bend,
We spy our journey's end.
We manoeuvre to the jetty, then step ashore
And there's the pub - we head for the front door.

We wait there for our absent friend to re-appear
And share our separate adventures - with a beer.
Then we ponder 'bout the weather and clear water.
What a shame she couldn't come -

>*she really should've oughta!*

*York is a beautiful city but is struggling under the pressure of
the huge number of tourists who flock there, mostly from
other countries without the good manners we have
(or had) and with little understanding
of the fairness of waiting
their turn.*

*This poem has been
written from the
viewpoint of
a resident -
not a tourist!*

# Aah, York!

Once headquarters
of the Roman Empire
And now the capital
of God's own Yorkshire.
Tourists crowd into historic places,
Have a trip on the river, have a day at the races,
Relax in the gardens or walk on the wall,
Or visit the Minster. *(It's not a cathedral).*

They can find out about Eboracum and Jorvik,
That is to say things that are Roman and Nordic.
They can see locomotives from the age of steam,
If they walk up the hill to the Railway Museum.
There are so many places where they can go,
Then can finish their day with a meal or a show.

The trouble with living in a tourist attraction
Is that everyone else wants a piece of the action.
It's good to see foreign tourists and we all need their cash
But they're not used to our ways so shouldn't be rash.
When we're waiting for service, they'll find that we queue.
If they push, if they shove, we'll take a dim view.

And when they get lost, they ask us the way
But can't understand a word that we say.
They link arms four abreast and march straight at us,
Whilst we try our best to keep out of the gutters.
They hunt in packs. They form such a throng.
It's quite a relief that they don't stay too long!

Things settle down when the coaches have left
And then empty streets appear strangely bereft.
Tomorrow morning it'll all start again
But let's look on the bright side . . . perhaps it'll rain!

---

*Winter can be a depressing and dark time so, when spring finally arrives, the increased warmth and colour are very welcome. With a clear blue sky and the warmth of the sun, the countryside gradually awakens. Young lambs prance about and all the birds start to patrol their territory and sing out their warnings to rivals or to attract a mate.*

*The white blossom of blackthorn is soon followed by the bright green of the hedgerows as new leaves appear but by then, in the fields, a new interloper has arrived.*

# The Yellow Menace

I gaze at green fields, tinged with pale lemon,
Brown hedgerows and blue sky . . . an earthly heaven.
But soon these softer shades are humbled by a harsher hue,
As oil seed rape invades to vanquish and subdue.

An incandescent army overpowers,
Carpeting the land with open flowers.
Hordes of yellow soldiers subjugate the fields
Now their vibrant colour is revealed.

The yellow menace spreads both far and wide -
It constitutes a blight on our sombre countryside.
For a while, the sea of fluorescence conquers all
But, as with any rise of empire, comes the fall.

For then the petals drop - their power is sated
And calm colours in the countryside are reinstated.
An end to Mother Nature's bane.
Our green and pleasant land returns again.

*As an island race, none of us lives very far from the sea and coastal towns have always held a fascination. Most have fond memories of seaside holidays - playing games on the beach, building sand castles and frolicking in the surf.*

*Now I'm an adult, I like to stroll on the seashore but I don't like crowds. When the sun shines, people flock there. Conversely, in bad weather, the beaches might be deserted . . . save for the odd hardy soul.*

*I may agree with the sentiments of this poem but I couldn't possibly be that selfish!*

# My perfect day

A clear blue sky's *not* good for me,
Dark clouds are what *I* want to see.
When storms approach, when skies turn grey,
My spirits lift: my perfect day.

Blot out the warmth from solar rays,
Create instead patchworks of greys.
Unleash bleak hailstones, strafe the bay.
Drive fragile visitors away.

Day trippers, dogs and children too
Will dash for cover. That's my cue.
The beach then empties just for me -
A mile of sand and endless sea.

Blow in dark clouds and hide the sun,
Divide the crowds, cause them to run.
Come thunder, lightning, wind and rain,
Chase all away, till none remain.

It's only when the sun *can't* shine,
That I can really call it mine.
When bitter wind chills to the bone,
*Then* will I wander
. . . *on my own.*

Salt spray bites
and wind blows raw.
I'm not downhearted, *give me more!*
Paddling in boots and roaming free -
That's where and when I long to be.

Then undercover, hot soup drinking,
With weary legs and eyebrows tingling,
I stand and watch as clouds disperse.
I see the tempo of the day reverse.

The chill departs - the sun breaks through
And now the day begins anew.
The crowds return to claim *their* bay.
But *my* spirits lifted
       . . . *perfect day!*

# TIMEFRAME

*I was brought up in a three storey house in the middle of the town. My parents were able to spare a room on the top floor for me to use as a playroom. My favourite comic of the time was The Eagle and my hero was Dan Dare.*

*One Christmas I was given a Dan Dare transmitter and receiver. It consisted of a huge plastic box with lots of dials which didn't do anything and a small plastic receiver (much like the early mobile telephones which appeared in the 80s).*

*It came with a long wire which my father attached to the walls and under the stair carpet and which led down to the kitchen on the ground floor. My mother could then call me up and tell me when tea was ready.*

*Those of us growing up in the 50s and 60s were very conscious of the wonder of space. TV programmes of the time included 'Lost In Space' and 'Fireball XL5'.*

*The following character is loosely based on the Flash Gordon episodes - which I'm sure I would have enjoyed in my younger days,*

*. . . had I been born a few years earlier.*

# The maiden voyage of
# The Silver Flash

Out into the vastness of a distant galaxy,
Sped the high-jacked craft of
        Captain Horatio Magellan Fanta-Zee.
The hero of the hour and many more beside,
Decorated universally, revered both far and wide.

But the captain had finally seen the error of his ways.
He'd seized his opportunity and escaped to outer space.
He'd come to realise he'd been the Emperor's pawn
And for the rulers of the Empire he felt nothing now but scorn.

Accurate, quick and agile – easily the best
But when it came to thinking he was nowhere near the rest.
Cap Hooray (as his admirers dubbed him) stood
        over seven feet tall,
Packed with bulging muscles but with little intellect at all.

In a fight, you'd want him on your side -
        a giant amongst men.
Strong as an ox, quick as a cat and fearless
        as a Tyleer Antellarian.
A small bird was his ally. She was his sole companion
His brawn, her brain combined to make
        a peerless combination.

His survival had depended on his green and yellow budgie
She'd got him out of several scrapes.
        He chose to call her . . . 'Budgie'.
They travelled together everywhere, never were they apart.
Though the Captain could be rather stupid,
        his bird was twice as smart.

If the Cap was in a pickle, she'd determine the way out.
She could see the bigger picture, she'd be the perfect scout
But Cap Hooray had got himself into another situation.
His anger with the empire had now reached its culmination.

The Emperor had decided to create a super ship
But the captain had dismissed its crew for the inaugural trip.
He'd fastened all the doors and assessed his new domain
But he hadn't got a plan. He'd simply
      not engaged his brain.

Though it had a proper name,
      The Silver Flash, as it was known
Had still to prove its virtue – it had never yet been flown,
*Well, not into space anyway!*
But who would want to take the risk?
      You guessed it . . . Cap Hooray!

Packed full of innovations was the Emperor's new toy
But all its features *now* were for the Captain to enjoy.
He gazed at the controls. What was he going to do?
It occurred to him that once again
he hadn't thought this through.

The ship had been built
for the Emperor,
who was only five feet two.
Cap Hooray would hit
his head on every doorway
he walked through.
And at the top of each door-frame
was very soon displayed
A head-shaped gap that Cap Hooray had
unintentionally made.

He had to crouch to peer through all of the portholes.
And his fat fingers were too clumsy when he tried
>    to turn the dials
Another disappointment was that all the seats
>    were far too small
The Captain was beginning to wish he hadn't gone AWOL.

Then Budgie settled on the ignition switch.
Somehow, she knew which switch was which.
He squeezed into the pilot's seat and turned the ignition key
In an instant it transferred tri-dimensionally.

The crowd had been astonished, one second it was there,
Then it disappeared completely – vanished – into thin air!
They came to the conclusion that The Flash had vaporised
But Cap Hooray was still alive – it had dematerialised.

It re-appeared in outer space
>    and though Cap Hooray was shaken,
All in all, he was well pleased with the risks that he had taken.
When the Cap was undecided, Budgie would point the way.
Once again his clever bird had helped to save the day.

But now the Captain had recovered, he found he was nowhere.
That is, nowhere he recognised – all he could do was
>    stand and stare.
The planets were displayed on his 4D visi-screen . . .
Galaxies and constellations no human eye had ever seen.

More revelations were to follow in the days that were to come,
As he adapted to surroundings – for his new life had begun,
Determined now to champion the oppressed,
>    the weak and poor!

But then The Silver Flash just vanished . . .
>    exactly as it had before.

*Cowboy and Indian films and television series were very popular when I was young. That was the era of John Wayne films and The Lone Ranger, Rawhide and Bonanza on TV.*

*The first animation film I ever made with my 8mm cine camera was about a cowboy whom I christened 'Red Rogers'. I created very simple movements using cowboys and indians on horses with their legs alternating between closed and open positions. I requisitioned my parents' dining table for the duration of the filming which turned out to be for quite a few weeks.*

*The mountains behind the action were made from boxes and packing covered with brown sheets. I've since had my old films converted to the DVD format and I'm amused by their shortcomings - especially the mountains which rise and fall as the characters pass by. The following story was inspired by the hero of that film.*

# Red Rodgers

Red Rodgers was a cowboy in the old Wild West
But Red had got a secret – he wasn't like the rest.
He'd built a reputation. He was handy with a gun,
That was many years ago in duels that he'd won.

But now his sight was poorer than it had been in the past,
He couldn't make out people, though he *still* was just as fast.
He *could* rely on sound to find where other people were,
Otherwise their details to him were just a blur.

Then one day a young stranger rode slowly into town.
He tapped Red on the shoulder and looked him up and down.
He sneered "So you're the great Red Rodgers -
> they call me Bill.
Just look at you - you wouldn't beat me now . . .
> you're old, over the hill".

"Old timer!" taunted Bill.
He was itching for a duel.
He tried to anger Red with words both harsh and coarse
But that had no effect . . . until he criticised Red's horse.

"OK, you've got your wish" Red said "I'll wait for you outside
Deriding my prize stallion - that's one thing I *can't* abide".
So thirty feet apart, they faced each other in the street.
Red listened most intently for the sound of young Bill's feet.

But Bill was very careful *not* to make a sound.
He was wise to Red's condition and
dropped quickly to the ground.
Red's bullet whistled overhead
And lodged into a barn instead.

Bill was spread-eagled on the floor
And now it was *his* turn to draw.
He called " I really like your hat
And I'll be shooting into that".

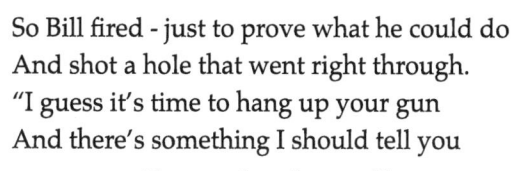

So Bill fired - just to prove what he could do
And shot a hole that went right through.
"I guess it's time to hang up your gun
And there's something I should tell you

> . . . *I'm your long lost son!"*

Red was dumbfounded at his cheek
But asked around – and in a week
He'd discovered that it was the truth.
He even traced Bill's Ma . . . called Ruth.

Bill's revelations changed Red's life,
For later Ruth became his wife.
Now Red's a *reformed* character -
He has a family, life is better.

Ruth keeps house, Bill goes to school
And Red? – he took instead to shooting pool.

---

*While I was living in London my flatmate and I formed a musical group which we called The Victoria Players to perform old Music Hall songs. It was a nod to the TV programme 'The Good Old Days'. We ran this group each winter season for five years. That's where I first met my wife who joined as a singer and dancer. She eventually became the choreographer and director when my flatmate moved on.*

*One year a large bearded gentleman dressed in a scout's uniform with short trousers and long socks arived at our front door to request an audition. He introduced himself as Ruxton Hayward. The most striking thing about him though was his very high voice - very reminiscent of Bluebottle in the Goon Show, voiced by Peter Sellers.*

*We realised eventually that it was his natural voice. He was a very confident eccentric. We gave him a spot in the show. Years later, we saw Peter Sellers on television recalling the person who had inspired Bluebottle's character - 'our very own' Ruxton Hayward.*

*When you're putting on a production, there are many things which can go wrong. I wouldn't want to take on all that stress again now.*

# The waiting game

Putting on a big show is a monumental task
For principals and backstage crew, for helpers and the cast.
But now, at last, the time we have been waiting for is near -
The show, which we all hope will be the highlight of our year.

We start to think - will everything we've worked for go to plan?
Will each of us do absolutely everything we can?
Will every uniform and suit and dress be stitched in time?
Will all the actors manage to remember every line?

Will every dancer know where they should be?
Will all the angelic singers sing in key?
Will all the props be in their proper place?
Will any hitches be prepared for just in case?

Will each and every person play their part?
For very soon performances will start.
But just remember, sadly, time moves on so fast.
Before we know what's happened,
      it'll all be in the past.

---

*Our class system, though much derided, is less evident than in medieval times when the ruling classes owned huge areas of land and the peasants were poor and downtrodden. Just below the lords and ladies in the pecking order were the knights.*

*We tend to think of that era as a glorious age of chivalry and honour but perhaps not all the knights were as honourable . . . and maybe not all the peasants were quite as simple.*

# A knight came a-riding

A knight came and folk asked "Who could he be?"
They all gathered round and clamoured to see.
He called out "A dragon lurks very near
But do as I say, there's no need to fear."

The villagers scoffed. "Who was he kidding?"
They wouldn't do what *he* was bidding!
A few days passed by, the knight was still there
But they *still* wouldn't listen, though he
laid his soul bare.

But then some things happened
 which seemed rather strange
And the villagers' mood was starting to change.
A cow went missing, two sheep were found dead,
Wives started to think they weren't safe in their bed.

They decided at last that the knight might be right
That's when they all thanked him for he offered to fight.
He addressed them again. This time they believed.
He'd go on his own. They were all most relieved.

The day soon arrived when his search was to start.
The shame-faced villagers loaded a cart
With their best weapons, meat, cakes and ale . . .
But a shepherd was curious and followed his trail.

After a while he caught up with the knight
Who'd made a camp fire. (He'd followed the light).
The shepherd was dumbfounded when he spied
The lost cows and sheep he'd managed to hide.

The shepherd rushed to divulge all that he'd seen -
About the knight and how deceived they'd all been.
They were furious and aghast!
Now, how to repay him? They had to think fast.

They made a huge dragon – from its nostrils gushed flame
And its head looked alive as it hung from a crane.
Some days later, the knight re-appeared
With a story to tell which he'd carefully prepared.

He rounded the corner and got such a fright.
A fire breathing dragon was ready to bite!
A monster so terrifying, it made his flesh crawl.
Coloured purple and green,
 it stood twenty feet tall.

The knight fled in panic,
flaming missiles whizzed past,
Whilst from far back behind him,
he heard a loud blast.
He ran and ran - he never turned.
'Twas his pride was most hurt
with a hard lesson learned.

Back in the village, peace and harmony returned:
Their adventure now over and rest was well earned.
Things settled down. Nothing new started.
No-one came near. No-one departed.

No news to tell you. No gossip was shared
But deep in the forest huge nostrils flared.
Two yellow eyes opened
        and sharp teeth were bared . . .

---

*Da dum di diddely dum di deeee . . . diddle di deeeee . . .
twang - whoosh - bonnngggg!*

*Anyone over the age of sixty will undoubtedly recognise that rhythm as the opening bars of 'The Adventures of Robin Hood' - one of our favourite TV series from the 1960s. He was a character who cocked a snook at authority - something we all want to do from time to time.*

*The English have a reputation for supporting the underdog. This tale picks out another character who could also have been regarded as the underdog.*

*Read it as if you were very, very cross!*

# Robin and a band of outlaws

*It's about that Robin Hood ... I'm filing a complaint.*
*You all think he's a hero. I can tell you that he ain't!*

I rue the day he deigned to join my merry little band.
It wasn't long 'fore things had got entirely out of hand.
What earthly use he'd ever be, I really couldn't see -
The only thing he brought us was a marketing degree.

He joined us as Lord Loxley but then he changed his name.
He knew the nickname 'Robin Hood' was
        bound to bring him fame.
He dressed us all in green tights with a little pointed hat.
The others liked his new ideas – so therefore that was that!

Bill Brown, Fred Took and Johnny Rand
Were the other outlaws in our band.
He changed their names,
now they're re-born
As Scarlet, Tuck and Little John.

He charmed his way into my gang
and changed it all completely
And now I'm on my own again.
He's turned my friends against me.
'Robin and his merry men' is now the brand new name.
I guess 'Obadiah Ramsbottom and his outlaws' ...
        isn't *quite* the same.

I don't like that Robin Hood – *he* only cares about himself.
My so-called friends desert me - and *I'm* left on the shelf.
But him? He's top dog with my chums!
They are a hopeless load of bums!

Stealing from the rich and giving to the poor
Would make us very popular, of that I was quite sure.
But that scoundrel Robin Hood, he stole my best idea
And he'll do it better than I did – he'll step it up a gear.

He's going to have to watch his back - he's made an enemy.
I'm determined. I'll not be beaten. He's met his match in me.
I'm bent on making mischief.
       He's got my pecker up - you'll see.
I'll get even. I'll be revenged. His nemesis I'll be.

I'm starting to see the other side, the Norman point of view.
I have some influential friends – I'll see what they can do.
I've heard elections for high office will very soon be due.
The voting will be taking place in just a month or two.

He'll be sorry. He's misjudged me: I'm a lion, not a lamb.
I'm going to be the sheriff . . .
    *the Sheriff of Nottingham!*

---

*Science fiction has always held a fascination for me. As a child, my favourite stories were about Dan Dare in the Eagle comic and The Trigan Empire in the Look and Learn and Ranger comics. My parents encouraged me to read Look and Learn as it was more educational but in those days I was more interested in looking at pictures than reading words. That bias carried through to my later career as a graphic designer.*

*My love of science fiction led me to be an avid fan of any time travel or space exploration adventure programmes on television - right from the first black and white episodes of Dr Who up to the recent Star Trek and Star Wars films.*

# It's about time

I wonder, if I had a time machine,
Where would I go? Where might I have been?
Would G forces make my limbs go numb,
If I slipped through the space/time continuum?

Could I explore the future or go back to the past?
My machine would have to work as fast,
If not faster than the speed of light.
How would I get the timing right?

If I wanted to see my team win the cup,
I might get there too late . . . as they were tidying up.
I could end up somewhere I hadn't planned -
Find myself in the ocean and not on dry land.

I could be Captain Kirk or perhaps Doctor Who
But would I win in the end, like they always do?
If I dematerialised and was lost in space,
There might be monsters I'd have to face.

Do I crave encounters of *any* kind?
No . . . I think I'll have to change my mind
And now I've started to lick my lips.
It's Friday – we're having fish and chips.

So *that's* the place I want to be.
I'm staying put

    . . . it's time for TEA!

*My favourite series of books is Isaac Asimov's 'Foundation' trilogy about the break-up and re-instatement of galactic empires. (The three books eventually turned into a series of seven). I've read all of them at least three times! The television series 'Blake's 7' had a similar theme, concerning a renegade band fighting another unjust galactic empire.*

*I suppose my image of 'Ced' derives from C3PO - the helpful 'butler' like robot in Star Wars. The name I gave him is a nod to Cedric, my alter-ego.*

# The Silver Flash flies again

The Captain took a long deep breath
    and then sat back and laughed.
He'd managed to escape with the Emperor's new spacecraft.
The ship was crammed with innovations –
    everything was new
But what the knobs and dials and buttons did,
    he hadn't got a clue.

He could dematerialise and transfer from place to place
But he needed to manoeuvre in a small volume of space.
The Captain sat and gaped at all the instruments before him
And wondered where in space
    would be the best place to begin.

He pressed a button. All the lights turned off:
    Complete and total darkness.
Somehow they came back on again. He carried on regardless.
He pressed the next one and his chair collapsed
    under the floor.
The Cap was losing patience - he pressed another three or four.

Then pandemonium ensued.
>The air was filled with rage and rants.
Budgie thought it might be wise to try and keep her distance.
The Silver Flash performed extraordinary acrobatics.
A frustrated Cap Hooray pressed yet another five or six.

It stuttered, looped the loop, and tilted quite a lot,
Then it spun into a spiral and oscillated on the spot.
Once it disappeared completely though it really was still there
But as the Captain was inside the craft - he just wasn't aware.

After that, it shrank a little - and then grew
But once again he couldn't see it, so he missed that too.
Inside the craft, the Cap was bumped and jerked and buffeted.
Rocked backwards and then forwards, rattled, rolled and jolted.

Meanwhile, as he shook and slipped and slid,
Budgie observed from her high vantage point - and hid.
Next the spacecraft travelled backwards
>and swayed from side to side,
Then the Captain cut the engines and simply let it glide.

Devoid of any motion, zero gravity ensued.
He duly floated to the ceiling. That didn't help his mood.
He never had enjoyed the experience of weightlessness.
He didn't have control -
>it just made him feel helpless.

Then he landed with a crunch. Gravity was suddenly restored.
Unfortunately, as he landed, he smashed through
> a circuit board.

Sparks flew in all directions. Smoke gathered in a plume,
Then the scene of devastation disappeared . . .
> as black smoke filled the room.

The Captain glowered at this further complication.
His gaze then drifted sideways to a shiny golden button.
It was oval and embossed with an ornate letter B.
He pushed but nothing happened . . . that is . . .
> not that he could see.

But a door dissolved behind him where stood
> the figure of a man.

"Greetings, excellency" he exclaimed
> "I'm here to serve you, if I can".

The Captain quickly turned around, his blaster in his hand -
He'd been convinced (when he'd first launched)
> that the spacecraft was unmanned.

And so it was, in essence, for the figure was robotic,
Bedecked in gold with face and hands of moulded neo-plastic.
Meant as a gift for the Emperor, regaled in full evening attire,
. . . and apparently dressed as a butler.
The Captain stood back to admire.

"Don't call me excellency"
said the Captain
"I've had enough of acquiescence
And lies and deceit and corruption.
The empire is full of that nonsense!
My own name's a bit of a mouthful
so just call me Cap'n instead
And I'll name you after my famous
great-great-great-great-great uncle Ced".

The robot looked dispassionately at the mayhem
> and destruction,
Then quickly set about an ordered reconstruction.
The robot knew about the ship and shared the details
> with his Cap'n.
Cap Hooray was so relieved to have Ced as his companion.

He started mending buttons and rushing here and there.
Ced also showed the Captain how to adapt a small armchair
And make it wider. Ced soon rectified the mess
> that the Captain had created,
Whilst the Cap collapsed into his comfy chair . . .
> and waited.

Then Ced said he'd heard a noise.
> He looked upwards to determine
What it was. He spotted Budgie and regrettably
> he called her vermin.
She'd watched the goings-on intently
> from her vantage point up high.
Incensed, she left a message all down
> his back as her reply.

So Ced and Budgie didn't start as friends -
> but the Captain had a word.
Ced acquiesced, and their hostility was thus deferred.
So when Ced had shown them both
> all that could possibly be shown,
They *all* set off together to *boldly* go
> to the unknown.

*Any event or story reflects the point of view of either just one person or a small group of people and that report could be a distortion of what actually happened. Looking back, maybe King Arthur wasn't as idealistic, perhaps King Canute wasn't as misguided and possibly King John wasn't as bad as they have all been reported. Any story, real or fictional, could always be viewed from a different perspective. Read this bit of nonsense in a sing-song voice.*

# Fray D'ah

I lives on me island in seclooshun,
Wid coconuts 'nd fruit 'nd fish in profooshun.
Waves lap on dee shore, palms sway in dee breeze.
Turquoise sea, *goulden* sand - me *own* paradees.

Id a mile long 'nd haff a mile wide
'nd a liddl bid more wen id at low-tiyeed.
Dare am wild goats 'nd crabs 'nd bananas galore
'nd sometimes a *sur-pryse* wid be washed ashore!

Me name's Fray D'ah. I liv on me-own.
Dat is, I *used* ta liv alone.
Back den, I had an *ee-zee* life.
Bud now me days, dey full of strife!

Tree wiks ago me spied a man on de shore -
A tall teene man . . .
me dared nat ignore.
I fallow'd hees
footprints in dee sand.
Just whoo wos
invadin
me wonderland?

Me diddin-no . . . he cud be hos-style,
I decidid ta kip a *low* pro-fyle.
Him climb up'n down, him loook here'n dere.
Him wanda aroune til hid bin *ebry-ware*.

He march inland, 'nd he clear a track
Den he startid ta build a makeshiff shack.
Me had tawt him may-be on'oliday
Bud . . . *now* id appeared him was plannin ta staye.

Den he *discover'ed* me one day.
Until den I'd managed ta kip ou'ta hees waye.
Now hee's wid me constantlee.
Me wish dat he would liv me bee!

Hee's repeatin 'nd repeatin "robson-kruus-inglis-maine".
I's starting to dink dat he may be insayne!
Hee's jabberin on abou dis'n'dat
Bud me? . . . me's nat inclyned ta chat.

Me can't understan any-tin hee's sayin.
I really hop hee's not dinkin of stayin.
Me's got ta admit dat he *climbin'* well
But dee ground am littered wid coco-nat shelz.

He bin droppin hee's rubbish ebry-ware.
Him don-evin care
A-bow da mess he liv be-hynd.
Me guess he dinks dat I don mynd.

He doesn' kip de island cleene
'nd he's upset Fray D'ah's routeene.
Me lyfe use-ta be so i-dillick 'nd carefree.
*He* can'd eeven say *me-name* correck-lee!

When I go fishin, he jus get in dee way
'nd me's *still* no idea wod hee's tryin ta say.
He simms ta dink dat he know best
Bud *dis* am *myland!* . . . Hee's merely da guest.

Id such a shayme dat hee's led him-seff go.
Hees clothes - dey tredbare at ta'nee 'nd ta'elbow.
Hees hair am too long - in nid of a trim.
'nd he cud do wid a shayve - him's lookin' quite grim.

He act as if I wore his *slave*.
Dat's nat a nice way ta bee-haive.
He can'd stay here - id's *my* island.
Me-wish I cud make him unda-stand.

De supplye boat wid soon be bak againe.
I's got till den ta ascertain
How ta pers-uayde him ta say gudbyee
'nd sail away . . . me gotta trye.

Him's a pain in da neck - he can't liv me alone.
I's just hopin he doesn' find ma *phone!*
Me bet he'd never giv id bak.
Dat man's a megalomaniac!

Hee's foreva wanderin to 'nd fro.
Hee's nat suited ta liv on dee archipelago.
I gotta hide him from all ma chums
'nd now I's worried n'case one comes.

If he meets da huntin, shootin 'nd fishin brigade
Ma social standin's bound ta fade
'nd him's sure ta gate-crash ma next soirée.
*How am I gonna kip him away?*

Ad's clear - me's gotta make a plan.
*Now . . . how am I go'in ta get rid of dis man?*

*The year goes by so fast and it's sometimes difficult to remember what happens when. I made notes throughout the year for this one - so it took quite a while to compile.*

# Month after month

*January*

The party's over - no more fireworks,
        toasts and midnight fun.
Now we can look forward for a new year has begun.
New year's resolutions made, new attitude -
Give up chocolate (again), more activity, less food.

But someone's got to finish off these sweets
And tins of biscuits and all the other treats.
I'll not worry 'bout iced buns and warm mince pies.
I'll eat them as I exercise!

Gritter lorries spread their load,
Abandoned cars wait to be towed.
While children get their longed for snow,
Frustrated drivers wish that it would go.

*February*

Sledging tumbles, snowball fights and slips on ice -
Put on extra clothes – much better to be wise.
We venture out with coat, hat, scarf and glove
And still it doesn't seem enough.

Fallen snow so quiet under bleak and distant sun
We revel in the scene but cold wind bites and ears go numb.
Dangerous icy pavements are comprehensively avoided,
Yet children slide with glee where others *fear* to tread.

With carrot nose and button eyes,
Snowmen suddenly materialise.
Until it thaws, they're loathe to go,
Till ice can melt and waters flow.

*March*

Winter's sombre monochrome views
Transform into contrasting hues.
Snowdrop and crocus bloom until
They bow to yellow daffodil.

End of winter, start of spring,
Now the birds will start to sing.
Daylight longer, night-time less,
Creatures of all sorts seek to impress.

Morning birdsong fills the air.
As each solitary bird seeks to become a pair.
Clocks move forward - more day, less night.
Spirits lift - now all seems bright.

But don't count chickens, no - not quite yet.
It's only March - let's not forget
That winter's chill still lingers on.
The risk of snow may not have gone.

*April*

Trees and shrubs enrich the scene -
So many different shades of green.
And offspring from the pregnant ewes
Gather in fields to share their news.

New life appears in many ways and in different guise,
On the ground and underground, in seas and in the skies.
Insects and animals awake from their long slumber
And birds and bees are adding to their number.

The brooding pigeons coo and coo and coo and coo
      . . . and coo and coo
I try to shoo them off my land. I prod at them
      with canes of bent bamboo.
If only I could reach, I'd run them through!

No of course I wouldn't kill them . . .
      *however much they coo!*

*May*

Life is good - but young animals learn to run
Because, for some, it's a short one.
For predators have got their own to feed,
If only for continuation of their breed.

Now colour returns to our rural landscape
As each tree and shrub increases its shape
Hedgerows are speckled white as if we've had more snow,
And now the fields are muted hues - or a bright yellow.

For 'twixt fields of sombre brown and green
An incandescent colour is now seen.
Where 'ere you gaze you won't escape
Ubiquitous crops of oil seed rape.

In gardens, tulips and climbers take their turn,
Followed by uncoiling stalks of fern
And fruit trees welcome spring with reds and pinks,
Rewarding energetic bees with nectar drinks.

*June*

As days get warmer, plans are made for weeks to come,
To escape the daily grind for sea and sand . . . and sun.
Some prepare to face the airport queues,
While others explore different avenues.

In London, tourists flock to see
The Trooping Of The Colour and Her Majesty
And, as the Wimbledon Championships begin,
Tennis fans debate which of the current stars will win.

*July*

If rain falls on St Swithin's Day,
Prepare for forty more – that's what they say.
And rain may fall on Wimbledon,
Before it comes to a conclusion.

School holidays then get underway
And children gather in the parks to play,
Or crowd into the centre of the town
Where they stroll aimlessly up and down.

*August*

Skimpy dresses, short sleeved shirts,
Even less for extroverts,
Though those with less of a physique
Might best be served to be more meek.

Shoulders sore and backs bright pink
For those who dared . . . but didn't think,
Who didn't care or just forgot
High summer sun could be that hot.

Bronze bodies exercise in longed for heat,
While others hide, white as a sheet
In shade from parasols where none can see
And sip cool drinks less hurriedly.

*September*

Once again, football results are on the News, so . . .
*'Look away now if you'd rather not know'.*
And autumn schedule previews appear on our TVs,
With another crowd of singing and dancing wannabees.

Farmers still watch the forecasts
        and strive to get their timing right,
So they can gather in the harvest when it's at sufficient height.
Tractors with their heavy laden trailers hurry to and fro,
Whilst hedgerows produce bountiful supplies
        of berry, hip and sloe.

With fiery colours, the trees bow out in style.
We shall not see their like for quite a while.
As a tired sun sinks lower in the sky,
We sense the season's end is almost nigh.

*October*

Indian summer turns to English autumn
        and the temperature drops,
Then Christmas gifts and decorations appear in all the shops
And seasonal songs and carols all continuously play.
It's far too soon – it's still two months away!

There's a chill in the air, wet leaves everywhere
And very soon the trees will all be bare.
Winter beckons and it's that time when
We forget to move our clocks back by an hour again!

*November*

Young entrepreneurs shout "Penny for the Guy".
Their efforts seem to be in vain as most pass by
But before long they have more coins than they can handle -
Enough to by some rockets, a Volcano
        and a Roman Candle.

We listen to the warnings 'bout how dangerous fireworks are
But some feel *it's the fun that's died* . . .
> Health & Safety's gone too far.
We must protect our pets of course
And keep them where it's quiet - and indoors.

We build bonfires out of branches, sticks and logs
But, before they're lit, we're asked to clarify there are
> no hedgehogs
Searching for a place to hibernate,
For their presence there would surely seal their fate.

*December*

Wide eyed children queue to sit on Santa's knee
"Have I been good?" they think "Will he remember me?"
Relatives and friends we rarely hear from get in touch
But do we want to read those long Round Robins –
> no, not much!

Shops are filled with people buying presents.
Will they be appreciated? Might they be disappointments?
Families transform their homes with tinsel, lights and tree
And some will go to church and bend their knee.

Then after all the hype and frenzy of the few weeks past,
Christmas Day arrives – it's here at last!
But, while films and TV Specials vie for our attention,
The reason for it all, God's son, will barely get a mention.

*Next . . .*

TV stations broadcast retrospective shows,
As yet another year draws swiftly to a close.
We've only just recovered from the Christmas parties, when
There's another celebration
> *and it's party time again!*

Old Father Time will vanish and a new year will appear.
We'll remember all our highs and lows and maybe shed a tear.
Then, at the end, a countdown to Big Ben's midnight chime.
We cross our arms and sing the half remembered words
... of Auld Lang Syne.

*The 1980s were a time of a revival for the English folk song and dance traditions. We were living in a village just south of Manchester and in 1981 we decided to form a Morris Dancing side called Handforth Morris. The side survived for about ten years.*

*People tend to think that English Morris dancers all wear white, dance with bells tied round their knees and wave hankies in the air. However, there are many variations of Morris. They include North East Rapper, East Midland Long Sword, Welsh Border Morris and the hankie one which is based in the Cotswolds.*

*Clog Morris originated in the North West area of England. That was the tradition we followed. Each year we invited other sides to join us to celebrate the patron saint of England - on St George's Day. We included a 'Mumming Play' which told the story of George's duel with the dragon. This poem, however, is an appraisal of our victorious knight by the dragon ... and this specific dragon was quite cultured. Read it with a pompous upper-class accent.*

# The dragon & George

I'd only been dozing for a few hundred years
When a dreadful commotion made me prick up my ears.
A horde of hoomans had come. They were making a racket.
I must say, they annoyed me - right from the outset.

Now I was awake I felt *awfully* peckish,
So I helped myself to some spicy shellfish.
I'm fussy 'bout food - I like my meals hot.
You could say I'm a bit of a gastronaut.

I like unicorn on the cob with some lean mammoth pie,
*Though the ingredients have lately been hard to come by.*
I was still hungry when I'd finished eating
When I heard an odd noise - a strange sort of bleating.

The sound echoed in from outside my lair.
Then a beast entered in wearing woollen knitwear.
It must have escaped from their stockade.
T'was delightful with a lemon and garlic marinade.

I was particularly partial to those woollen beasts.
And started having regular feasts.
Each week they'd leave one not far from my cave.
At least that was a considerate way to behave.

Then, when all the woollen beasts had gone,
They left me female hooman-beans to feed on.
They weren't nearly as tasty - not as much of a treat.
Though I shouldn't complain ... simply not enough meat!

I've got to admit that it didn't seem right
To devour their young maidens - though I say this in hindsight
But it would have been churlish to refrain
I've a reputation to maintain.

Now . . . who's this approaching my lofty lair?
Another fair maiden with silky blond hair?
No, it's a haughty young man astride a white hoss
Sporting a white tabard with an embroidered red cross.
*Mmm, quite nicely done.*

Have they run out of virgins for me to digest?
And sent him instead . . . can't say I'm impressed.
They'll have to understand that this'll
Not do - I simply *can't* eat meat with a load of gristle!

Oh dear, I've developed an excess of gas
And it's building into quite a large mass.
**BOOOAR-R-R-R-R-H !**
Whoops, his hoss reared up. He's been thrown
And now he's standing there all alone.

He pontificates, waving his sword about.
I think he's itching for a bout.
Does he *really* mean he wants to fight?
I shouldn't laugh but it's
a surreal sight.

His heavy chain-mail glints in the sun.
I think it's time to have some fun.
He must be cold - his knees are shaking.
I'll share some warm breath. It's time to start baking!

He jabs with his sword, in and out, here and there.
I launch an attack with projectile hot air.
*I like hooman-beans toasted with a little cheese -*
*To be more precise 'au gratin' if you please.*

He's quite adept with his sword - and with his spear.
He tries to get close but he's still nowhere near.
Now he's shouting - "Blah-di-blah-di-blah-di-blah".
This situation's so bizarre.

He thinks he'll impress with his swashbuckling style.
I'll shower him with sparks - keep him busy a while.
I'm determined he won't get the better of me.
Now my nose is itching - *ATCHOOOOO!!!!*
 . . . *Oh what a shame! . . . I liked that tree.*

We continue to duel back and forth, to and fro.
I won't let him reach but he has a good go.
Now he's waving his sword . . . and he's increased the tempo.
I have to admit, he puts on a good show.

*But I'm not doing so well!* I might beat a retreat,
'Cos now I'm not sure that I can compete.
He's seen that I'm flagging - I've had so much to eat.
He's wearing me out and I need to re-heat.

He's surprisingly strong and quite an athlete
And he's such a good mover - so light on his feet
But he can't possibly reach *that* far.
Now, if I can just . . .
 . . . *a a a a a a r g h !!!!*

*116*

*We can be quite cynical when watching a drama on TV or in a film. We've got used to seeing the point at which the hero is in a fix from which he can't possibly escape. We'll turn to each other and and exclaim "Things are looking pretty black!" Cap Hooray was about to reach that point.*

*The Cap had got used to his new spaceship and was having fantastic adventures - but even superhuman spacemen have to eat . . .*

# The return of The Silver Flash

Five weeks away from earth and food supplies
    were running low
Cap Hooray had made his plans –
    he knew where he must go.
Huge cargo ships would speed through space
    almost every day
From the hydroponic farms on Mars –
    they should be easy prey.

The Captain's favourite steaks would be stored
> by the bulkhead.
There would be seed for Budgie too -
> at least that's what Ced said.
So Ced keyed in co-ordinates, The Flash vanished from view,
When they materialised near Mars,
> the ships were waiting in a queue.

They engaged invisibility and edged close to the convoy,
Hoping that no-one would spoil their bold audacious ploy.
The Captain donned his helmet
> and turned his blaster down to 'stun'.
The Flash then parked alongside 'Cargo-Ship Six Forty One'.

They locked on to the docking bay and quickly got inside.
The plan went well. They'd left almost as soon
> as they'd arrived.
They collected all they needed. They never saw the crew.
There was *no-one* to challenge them as swiftly
> they passed through.

They'd returned onboard The Silver Flash
> before they'd been detected -
A successful raid but food supplies
> weren't all that they'd collected.
For a stowaway had crept inside and was waiting by the door.
"Cap Hooray" the stranger said "So, it *was* you that I saw".

They faced each other motionless, both with
their blasters drawn –
The Captain and his nemesis,
the notorious Pirate Dawn.
"I see you're still alive" said Dawn
"despite what we've been told
And now with a robotic man -
entirely made of gold!"

Dawn was a top tactician, everything the Captain wasn't.
While he'd rely on speed, she'd tend to be more reticent.
Dawn lived by her wits, the Cap would use brute force.
He'd always make the obvious choice, she'd choose
>	a different course.

The Captain charged at Dawn but remarkably
>	ran right through.
Dawn had anticipated precisely what he'd do.
Her image was unaltered - it was a hologram, you see.
He'd obviously been hoodwinked.
>	*So, where in space was she?*

He'd ended in a heap - his head embedded in a door.
Then the Cap was on his feet
>	to find what else she had in store.
He turned to see the image of her smug rejoicing face.
As Budgie hovered overhead . . . *above Dawn's hiding place!*

The Captain aimed his blaster and a wall dissolved entirely.
Dawn was suddenly exposed and finally at his mercy.
She had lost the fight - the Captain was victorious
But our hero Cap Hooray then did
>	something oddly curious.

He knelt down and very carefully placed
>	his blaster on the floor.
"A gesture of good will" he said
>	"I'll not fight you anymore".
"I've seen the light" the Captain said
>	"It seems you were right all along -
The Empire's rotten to the core.
>	I admit that I was wrong".

"So tell me Pirate Dawn, will you join me in the fight
To tackle all injustices and make the wrong things right?"
Dawn wondered if he'd really changed -
    and was she wise to trust him,
Or was this just a ruse and yet another sneaky scheme?

She pondered 'bout which course to take for a little while.
"No, just take me to my *own* spaceship"
    she answered with a smile
But when the time to transfer came,
    she simply changed her mind.
She trapped the Captain in her ship and then left him behind.

But would the Captain's two compatriots
    arrive to rescue him?
Sadly they were unaware of the mess that he was in.
Whilst Ced performed an oil change,
    Budgie nibbled on a grape.
The Cap was on his own this time - no chance of an escape.

Dawn's craft was small and basic and in a sorry state
But the Captain had no time to think about this twist of fate.
With its armoury depleted and severely battle scarred,
He'd have to quickly settle in - and then be on his guard.

Then two spaceships from the Empire arrived and opened fire.
Cap Hooray was in a fix – his circumstances dire.
His only viable weapon was the astrotomic ray
But, though he tried to use it, he was just too far away.

Then with their second salvo they destroyed his last torpedo
And now there was no firepower left
    with which to fight his foe.
His defensive shield was down with power
    at only five per cent,
Marooned, in limbo, helpless, his oxygen near spent.

Cap Hooray was desperate - things were looking pretty black
As the enemy repositioned to start their next attack.
But just as things were looking at their very worst
The airlock opened . . . and it was Dawn who
      through the hatchway burst.

Dawn had watched it all. She'd not believed his true intent
But his actions proved that what he'd said to her he'd meant.
"The Flash has stayed connected,
      though we vanished from your view.
We never disengaged" she said
      "I had to see what you would do."

"I've been chatting to your metal man and maybe I was rash,
So will you come aboard - *and join me* on The Flash?"
Of course, he was relieved to venture back aboard
And he understood what Dawn had done –
      mutual trust was now assured!

They'd only just departed when Dawn's ship was torn in two
As the empire ships deployed a hyper-periton lasso.
Their enemies thought they'd seen the end
      of the dreaded Pirate Dawn.
They never guessed that (like the captain)
      she would *also* be reborn.

The Silver Flash would venture now where
      only few could tread,
Now with a crew of three amigos . . .
      that's the Captain, Dawn and Ced

*. . . and Budgie of course.*

# ON THE MOVE

*Nowadays, most opportunities for work are to be found in the cities or larger towns but buying a house in these areas can be expensive. Consequently, many workers live at a distance and have to travel to work every day.*

*I worked in York for a while whilst living in a village just outside Scarborough. Every morning I'd stand on the platform at Seamer station waiting for the train to arrive. We're generally creatures of habit and most of my fellow travellers would wait in the same spot - as I did.*

*Some of the regulars had struck up friendships and would huddle together but most of us would stand on our own. We were all lost in our own separate worlds, sitting or standing, reading or tapping on a mobile phone or just staring at nothing in particular and thinking.*

*This is a slightly screwy interpretation of the daily routine experienced by commuters.*

## Off the rails

I find myself staring at the rails again,
Then look up, to search for a train . . .
There's no train. My gaze returns to the track.
The track stares back.
Both motionless and lost in reverie:
Transfixed, the railway track and me.

The track: small but vital, yet to everyone unseen . . .
And me: a minor cog in a vast human machine.
My fellow statues stir, in anticipation
Of yet another routine journey to a well-trod destination
And then the train materialises. Squeaking wheels rush by.
The portal to our next location opens with a sigh.

Twenty four hours race past. We each find our usual place,
All of us participants in a half-hearted human race.
The same faces are here, the same briefcases, shoes and hats,
Whilst, below the platform, still the railway tracks
Wait for iron wheels. I wait for a door.
I get the same reaction as before.

Again time passes - but, today, there's something new:
A bunch of flowers has appeared to brighten up the view.
Maybe someone had a sad occurrence here
        and its been left as a reminder.
Maybe a distressed lover threw it in a fit of temper.
The wrapping paper caresses my piece of track
        and waves - as if to me:
A small movement where utter stillness had been
        all that I could see.

The train appears again. We wait in readiness.
The track and I exchange a wave . . . well, more or less.
The carriages edge past. A door arrives in front of me.
It signifies an end to this brief moment of serenity.
Once again the doors all sigh, then calmly open wide.
My adversaries scramble to be first and rush inside.

I sigh, *myself*, now we've departed,
For the busy-ness of life is impatient to get started
And the moment's gone.
        . . . Time to move on.

*My parents bought an old car for me when I was seventeen. I'd managed to pass my test at the first attempt and I enjoyed the independence and the thrill of driving at speed. I can still remember my mother's reaction when I told her I'd done a ton on the motorway. How could I be so naive?*

*On another occasion, I drove a new girlfriend to a show in London after which we walked back to the car only to discover that it wasn't there anymore. I'd parked on a zig-zag line near some traffic lights and eventually discovered that it had been towed away. She wasn't impressed. You won't be surprised to learn that we didn't go out again.*

*I've been driving a car for about fifty years now. Like most young whipper-snappers I used to break the speed limit occasionally but as I've got older I've slowed up quite a bit. After about twenty years without any points on my licence, I was incensed to get stopped for doing thirty eight in a thirty limit. The topography was obviously that of a forty limit (except that it wasn't).*

*The police were lying in wait in a side road, behind a six foot high brick wall. Shortly after that, my wife was caught in similar circumstances . . . no, not lying behind a brick wall.*

# Over the limit

When I'm out in my car, I drive *quite* fast
But *wherever* I go I'm often passed
By speeding cars going faster than *me!*
Speed restrictions they don't see.

They rush through our village at *such* a speed.
No warning signs will they *ever* heed.
A 30 sign has now appeared in it,
Which lights up if you exceed the limit.

I doubted the frequency would abate
If all it did was illuminate
And drivers continue to rush right through,
So the Police are trying something new.

They lie in wait – you don't know they're there,
Then they zap you with a speed gun – now that's not fair!
To light up the sign I thought would be fun.
I didn't *see* them there - with their zapping gun.

They hid round a corner so I couldn't see
And now I've incurred a penalty
And I also have to pay a fee.
A cheeky chap I thought I'd be
Till I was caught

. . . *now the laugh's on me!*

*I've done a lot of travelling to and from my work place by train and I've filled the journey times by either reading a book or writing the odd verse. This has had a cathartic effect - it's enabled me to cope with the annoying antics of some of the people with whom I've had to share a carriage.*

# My fellow passengers

The mobile user who shouts "I'm on the train"- oblivious!
We have to listen . . . but no-one makes a fuss.
The teenager who never blows his nose and sniffs
    every five minutes or so.
The woman talking loudly and sharing what should be secret.
    She doesn't care if we all know.
He sniffs again. I wish he'd go.

That tinny sound from headphones that everybody hears.
He'll probably be deaf in just a few more years.
The schoolchildren (who all sit on the floor)
Talk over one another, just a little to begin with,
    then later more and more.
Another sniff. Has no-one ever told him
    what a handkerchief is for?

People who don't care about the lingering smell
    from heated food like pasties,
Chicken curry or fish and chips . . . with peas.
When they go, they leave their messy packaging behind,
Or stuff it out of sight for someone else to find.
There's no consideration. They should *all* be fined.

Then there's the toddler who screams when he first sees the sea.
I try to show them how they ought to be.
But we don't see these things the same -
    the passengers and me.
Why can't they watch the countryside go by?
    Why don't they look?
Can't they read a magazine or a book?

He sniffs again. I offer him a paper handkerchief.
He gives *me* a funny look!

*I'm very set in my ways. I like cycling and I was very fond of the thirty year old bike which I 'borrowed' from my wife a good few years back. It had been hand painted to cover up all the rust and had a wicker basket under the handlebars. I did feel a little embarrassed about the basket and replaced it with a plastic one when I started riding to work. I decided it was time to part company when the squeaky noises got too annoying.*

*I really did exchange the old bike for a new model which had a complicated gear system but I've exaggerated the rest of the poem.*

# I've got a new bike

I've got a new bike. Well, actually it's second hand
But it's new to me! My excitement I hope
        you'll understand.
It's got wide tyres and it's painted blue.
What do you think? It is *almost* new.

You change gears with your left hand
        and then with your right
And it's shiny and modern and ever so light
But with too many gears from which to decide!
All I really want is a carefree ride.

I had my *last* bike for thirty years.
It was rather rusty - with just three gears.
I'm not sure how *these* gears operate
But to go for a ride – well, I just can't wait.

I've transferred the lights and got a wide cushioned saddle.
My bum is slightly wider and that'll
Suit me just fine.
I'm going to have a glorious time!

But I don't use my bike when conditions aren't right.
When it's snowing, icy, raining, foggy, too hot,
          too cold, windy
                    ... or at night.
It's too dangerous. I'm sure I'm making the right decision
And I want to look after my new acquisition.

I really miss my old apparatus
But I'm aware that I used to make a fuss.
Now I'm not sure exactly what to do.
Time's moved on and it's all so new.

I'll stay inside and bide my time.
I'll go out for a ride when the weather's fine.
No, really - I'm just waiting for the sun to shine ...

---

*Natural mineral waters were discovered in Scarborough in the 1620s and in the early 1700s a spa house was built there. It became very fashionable for people to drink from the spa's waters in order to improve their health.*

*Before very long it was popular to bathe in the sea and visitors also enjoyed boating and horse racing on the beach. The town grew in popularity.*

*We live near York and we often go to Scarborough for a day out as it's our favourite seaside destination. We've had many happy days there.*

*Some days will always remain memorable - but not necessarily for the reasons we might expect.*

# Cedric's special day

Cedric and Minnie Fitzwilliam
Had grown tired of their breaks in the sun.
English towns now seemed inviting,
So they looked at a map and chose one.

The town they decided to visit
Was York . . . and the places nearby.
Min said they should go to the seaside.
At that Cedric gave a deep sigh.

He'd been born and brought up
in Scarborough
And recalled younger days
on the shore.
It didn't mean much
to poor Minnie -
She'd not been
to Yorkshire
before!

It seemed that they waited for ages
Till the date of their holiday came.
Then they finally stepped onto the platform at York
With two cases and Min's
Zimmer frame.

They looked round the Minster,
Spent a day at the races,
Toured museums and shops -
All the usual places.

Next was their trip to the seaside.
And Cedric's big day had arrived.
As their train pulled into the station
He looked at his wife misty-eyed.

They decided to hire a deckchair,
Then they sat down and gazed out to sea.
(Cedric reliving his lost youth)
Minnie just let him be.

In his mind, he was still young and vibrant
And said he was fed up with sitting.
He jumped up and announced that he'd go for a swim.
Min carried on with her knitting.

Cedric threw off his clothes to reveal
A swimsuit which Minnie had knitted,
In an old fashioned style from shoulder to knee.
(He was truly amazed that it fitted).

He marched right up to the water,
Ducked down and then started to swim.
He sped off towards the horizon.
Thinking it might
impress Min.

But when
he turned round
he went backwards.
The current was stronger than he.
The tide was now flowing against him.
Unbeknown, he'd been swept out to sea.

Cedric was starting to worry.
His limbs were beginning to tire.
He wished that he'd not been so reckless,
When he realised he'd swum out
so far.

Back on the beach, Min sat knitting,
When she witnessed a startling sight.
Her wool was unravelling quickly,
So she tugged it with all of her might!

It was then that he felt something pull him.
He reached down and held on for dear life.
He gripped with what strength he could muster
And cut through the surf like a knife.

Min's wool was attached to his swimsuit.
As she tugged, he was pulled back to shore
But his costume was slowly diminishing.
With each tug he lost a bit more!

He got back to dry land not quite naked,
For the costume still covered a knee.
"I wasn't worried 'bout him when I pulled it -
That wool was expensive" said she.

A crowd of onlookers gathered -
At this he went red in the face.
Then Min looked around and passed Cedric his hat,
Which he held in an opportune place.

They asked: "Would she be
knitting more swimsuits?"
She retorted:
"The likelihood's slim!
You can bet that
whatever I make next,
*It won't be a swimsuit
for him!"*

*Regular railway commuters get to know where their chosen door will stop when the train pulls up. Accordingly, they'll usually wait in the same place on the platform.*

*It's not a foolproof art . . . but that's where the game comes in.*

# The double door game

Arriving on the platform, players choose
        their best position.
We'll soon find out which one of us has made
        the best decision.
It's a game that most of us will play.
Where will the double doors end up today?

Some chat with friends. Some stand alone.
Some play those stupid games on mobile phones.
Some banter loudly with their mates.
Whilst others quietly berate.

But, when the train's been sighted,
        their laid back attitude's *not* the same.
They jostle for position. We begin to play the game.
Some judge its speed and move accordingly
And some rely on past experience (like me).

Sometimes the train's arrival is quite fast.
        At other times it's slow.
Nonetheless it usually stops
        in *roughly* the same place . . . I know!
I stand my ground but some walk on. It rushes past.
Who'll end up first and who will be the last?

For whoever gets on first can choose
From all the empty seats. The others lose!
They must accept the second choice, or third,
    or fourth, etcetera
And then just hope that next time they'll do betterer.

The train draws to a halt and I've misjudged *completely!*
It's gone too far. My adversaries crowd in front of me.
Are there empty seats inside? I can't quite see.
I'm at the back. *That's not where I should be!*

It's all the driver's fault.
    He should have come in more sedately.
After all, that's how he has approached the platform lately.
Anyway, there usually is a vacant seat. There may be more
And I find out . . .
    when I pass through the double doors.

---

*Many people are scared of spiders but how might they feel about larger animals like lions or bears . . . or wolves?*

# Humpty & Miss Muffet

Humpty Dumpty sat on a wall.
He didn't hear Miss Muffet's call.
A spider scared her. She ran away.
But where she went no-one could say.

All the King's horses marched up and down.
The soldiers scrambled and searched through the town.
Three minutes later she'd still not been found,
Though everyone looked - they searched all around.

Humpty stood on his wall and peered out to sea,
No-one on the seashore - where could she be?
He scanned the dry land away from the ocean
And in a field far away saw such a commotion.

By a ramshackle house made entirely from sticks,
Two little pigs were making their exits.
A wolf on its knees was gasping for air
And the two pigs inside had had quite a scare.

Nearby Humpty noticed a large pile of straw
But then there was something else that he saw.
He looked more intently for just behind that
Quivering and shaking was Miss Muffet's hat.

She was confused and alarmed - considerably more
Than the spider had scared her just minutes before.
They rushed over to help her get to her feet.
Now our story is very nearly complete.

Humpty thought they should celebrate.
    They were bound to agree.
So Polly put the kettle on and they all had some tea.
Then for a fine egg-shell finish they erected a tent
All their friends were invited to a special event.

The owl and the pussycat and Wee Willie Winkie,
Little Bo Peep and Georgie Porgie,
Miss Muffet and Humpty and all the King's men
Were relieved to be back together again.

*Thankfully, a rail journey is not normally interrupted for any length of time - but, when an interruption does occur, the passengers are rarely told what's going on.*

# An unexpected stop

The train slows to a stop. We all look up.
    It's pitch black outside.
No sign of life, no platform, just countryside.
Time passes and eventually the conductor has
    something he can say.
He apologises and then reveals a reason for the long delay.

It seems that there's a trespasser on the line
And all the trains behind are also at a standstill.
    Catching him may take some time.
Most of the passengers are glued to their IT equipment
    or they're tapping on a mobile phone.
They're wired for sound and vision,
    lost in a world of their own.

Meanwhile, those of us still in the real world are subjected
    to the dreadful sounds of a child's plaything.
Monotonous and saccharine sweet.
    It's really most annoying.
'The wheels of the bus go round and round' and 'Row, row,
    row your boat' etch themselves into my brain.
It's keeping one child very happy ...
    but it's driving me *insane!*

"How long will we have to endure that sound?
I wish the wheels of *this train* would start to go round!"
Well, eventually the trespasser is caught
        and once again they do
But this incident has led me to a curious point of view . . .

That one man can overload the system
        with such ease
And our fragile time-keeping schedule
        is soon brought to its knees.
The smallest change can overload the system
        and upset the status quo
And consequently our train (and others in a line behind)
        are running slow.

This little incident was insignificant
        and merely a brief irritant
But even so,
        *it makes you think . . .*

---

*I never had any interest in gardening until my wife and I bought our first house. From that moment the appeal grew for both of us. We started going to the RHS Garden Shows, though we have never made the effort to visit the show at Chelsea.*

*This poem was started during a long coach trip to 'Gardeners World Live' at the NEC, near Birmingham. Most of us share a sense of decorum when speaking in a public place and lower our voices accordingly.*

*However, there are others who don't !*

# The coach trip

Waiting at a pick-up point
        on our way to see a show . . .
Why are we still here?
        We should have left some time ago!

The inevitable latecomer
        climbs aboard - at last
And braves the piercing glances
        as she quickly marches past.

Now we're moving and we revel in
        the English country scene:
Forests, fields and farms -
        so many shades of green.

But from the seat behind us
        drifts an excited chattering voice.
She's even drowning out the
        background music noise!

Two hours it takes to get there
'cross many a hill and dale,
Rocking and rolling back and forth
along a winding trail.

I hope it will be worth it -
and that it doesn't rain
For on the journey back
we've got that voice
to face again!

*We've always been interested in steam trains and were very excited to get the chance to see The Flying Scotsman after its ten year renovation costing £4.2 million. It was designed by Sir Nigel Gresley as part of the A1 class – the most powerful locomotives used by the railways at that time. It was originally built at Doncaster in 1923.*

*We thought that would be an excellent place to see it, as it progressed on its way north to York.*

*It might even stop for a while.*

# The day we went to see The Flying Scotsman

We arrived at Doncaster station
        with plenty of time to spare.
Finding the best place to stand and wait
        was going to take some care.
The platforms were heaving with crowds of old men,
Each with a story of the days - way back when.

I spied a gap and claimed my ground
Determined to ward off chancers from the space I'd found.
Many tales were being told by enthusiastic spotters:
Older men and women with grandsons . . .
        and some with granddaughters.

I spent some time chatting with a young man and his son
I told them all about its hundred miles an hour run
And many other interesting details.
Then the little boy tugged at his father's coat-tails.

He glanced up at me and he smiled.
A most engaging cheerful child.
But what he whispered made me sad
"Is that The Fat Controller dad?"

An hour passed and still we waited.
The platform became more populated.
Someone said it had been delayed.
I felt my enthusiasm fade.

I shuffled impatiently with a sour face
Elbowing upstarts from my personal space.
Meanwhile my wife (trying in vain to keep warm)
Marched vigorously up and down the platform.

"Stand back from the edge" the announcer implored.
Her repeated request was roundly ignored.
The crowds did retreat as policemen approached
But behind them the gap was swiftly encroached.

The odd lummox stood on the edge and leaned forward.
Then behind him the crowd moved in similar accord.
Everyone wanted to get a good view.
If you had been there you'd have wanted one too!

Then someone spotted a cloud of smoke -
    or maybe it was steam.
An air of excitement echoed as we woke
    from our daydream.
The moment of truth at last was here!
And a hushed silence fell as The Scotsman drew near.

I focused my camera on an area of track
I knew what to do. I'd learned a knack.
I expected it would slow to a gentle crawl.
I'd get a sharper image as it rumbled past us all.

But it thundered through the station
>    at what must have been full power!
It could have been travelling at over
>    seventy miles an hour.
No majestic processional as it slowed to pass by.
No acknowledging our reverence –
>    just a *"Hello"* and *"Goodbye"*.

I pressed the trigger, then looked up
>    as carriages sped past.
I didn't see The Flying Scotsman -
>    *it came and went so fast!*
The moment I had waited for so patiently had gone.
So ended the final chapter of my standing marathon.

I checked my camera next to see what I had got.
Was I pleased to see the picture? No, I wasn't, not a jot.
When I looked down at my masterpiece,
>    I could see I'd been a duffer.

All I'd captured was the platform, some people . . .
>    *and a buffer!*

*Clacton and Walton were our closest seaside resorts when I was growing up in Sudbury and we spent many happy times there. Both piers were thriving centres of entertainment. My parents would play bingo and spend time in the amusement arcade. I preferred the ghost train and the dodgems.*

*Clacton also had a theatre on the pier. We saw a very slim Roy Hudd on stage there when he was just starting out. Other showbiz stars also progressed from the nearby Butlins site at Clacton to start their careers in the theatre on the pier.*

*Cedric and Minnie's visit to Clacton was a memorable day out for both of them but one which Cedric would rather forget.*

# Cedric and Min go to Clacton

Cedric and Min won't forget the day
That they spent at Clacton On Sea.
The weather was perfect with a mild sea breeze.
It started so happily.

They'd prepared everything on the previous day,
Slept soundly and woke up refreshed.
They arrived at the station in plenty of time
And caught the right train - who'd have guessed?

Min found a good seat by the window,
Took her coat off and started to knit.
Cedric pushed her zimmer up in the rack,
Till . . . eventually . . . he got it to fit.

He'd noticed a sign on the doors which read
'Smile, you're on CCTV',
So he started to look for the cameras
But never found where they might be.

As the lady on the speaker suggested,
He strolled up and down in each carriage,
Spotting the exits and safety equipment
And checking that no-one left baggage.

But when she started repeating herself,
He looked up and started to mutter.
"We're not stupid – don't treat us like children!" he said.
Min said "Shut up, they'll think you're a nutter!"

When they arrived, Cedric made for the prom
But Min made her intentions quite clear,
As she hitched up her zimmer frame
onto her back
And doggedly
marched to
the pier.

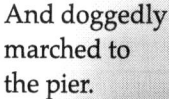

Min took her
zimmer frame with her
On all of the rides she went on.
She wasn't prepared to leave it behind,
Then afterwards find it had gone.

It helped get her onto her horse,
When they went on the merry-go-round,
Up the steps in the big helter-skelter,
Held aloft on her lap coming down.

Min had a go on the dodgems.
Cedric said *he* wasn't keen.
He went off to search for the toilets.
(Minnie had already been.)

In the opposite direction to everyone else,
Min flushed with unbridled power.
Cedric winced as he witnessed the
havoc she caused
And all at just two
miles an hour.

Minnie was
having a glorious time,
Ramming all of the cars in her way
But, for her wild and reckless behaviour,
She ought to have known that she'd pay.

It was then a boy-racer called Trev
Caught her corner and made the car spin.
The others all steered their cars out of her way.
That might suit the others - not him!

Min's walking frame fell from her passenger seat -
It landed in front of his bonnet.
Steering was useless – Trev's wheel wouldn't turn.
He couldn't help but drive on it!

It provided enough lift to enable his car
To launch itself into mid air.
It then came to rest in the midst of the crowd -
It gave all of them quite a scare.

Then, whilst attendants re-instated the car,
A sad Cedric looked on in dismay.
He subconsciously reached for his wallet
As he thought 'bout what he'd have to pay.

Min took it all in her stride -
"That ride was exciting" said she
But after he'd looked at the trail of destruction,
He wasn't inclined to agree.

He thought they'd be safe playing Bingo
But Min got the numbers all wrong.
She couldn't quite hear what the caller was calling.
Once again they were told to move on.

On the rifle range, perched on the rung of her frame,
Min was able to get a good view.
"The shelf shouldn't be quite so high" she said
"Cos I'm only four feet two!"

All the same, all her shots missed the target
But then she gave Cedric a stare.
He'd learned how to shoot in the army
And was handed a huge teddy bear.

By now they were feeling quite hungry
And they searched high and low for a seat.
They eventually found a suitable place
So they sat down and started to eat.

Cedric placed his big prize at the end of the bench
But then Minnie was slightly unkind,
For when he had finished he turned round to face her
And she laughed at his bear behind.

One or two hungry seagulls descended.
Min offered them some of her cake
But then other birds came to share in the spoils.
That turned out to be a mistake!

They made their escape in a hurry,
Then agreed they could do with a rest
And after all the excitement that morning
Thought a matinee film might be best.

They soon settled down without further mishap
And Min thought the film was enthralling
Though Cedric, tired after all that they'd done,
Fell asleep and then started snoring.

Then came a tense and dramatic scene,
Where the hero was trapped on a cliff
And Min, who was perched on the edge of her seat,
Stared wide eyed and went cold - and then stiff.

In despair, she stood up and shouted:
*"WON'T SOMEONE HELP?*
    *- HELP HIM SOMEONE!"*
Cedric sank lower in his seat
And then put his sunglasses on.

Soon after that the film ended.
They agreed they should call it a day,
For the clear blue sky of the morning
Had now turned quite cloudy and grey.

They were tired when at last they got home,
Though Min said she'd had a great day!
Her husband's retort was explicit
And I think it's not wise to relay.

But they felt that something was missing.
The day didn't seem somehow complete,
Till Cedric went into the garden
And he knew when he looked at their seat.

. . . Meanwhile, on a seat at the end of the pier,
Sat their teddy bear wearing a frown.
In the failing light, he sat all alone
And gazed at the sun -
going down.

# LOOKING BACK

*We all seem to change our opinions as we get older. I've recently noticed I'm saying things that I remember my parents saying, such as "Pop music today - you can't hear the words" and "These comedy programmes are just not funny". However, I don't feel any more mature now than I was then. Long may it continue!*

## The old days

Perhaps I won't notice the dust when I'm old
But I wonder will I feel that it's always too cold?
Will I go on 'bout *the old days* and things in the past?
Nowadays time seems to go by so fast.

Will I like classical music and swirly carpets?
Will my medicine cabinet be full of tablets?
Will I want the TV on too loud?
Will my straight back then be bent and bowed?

Will I love to boast 'bout my considerable age?
Will I be lucid? Will I be sage?
Will I go on 'bout *the old days* or relish the present?
Will I be decisive or . . . . . hesitant?

Will I get pleasure from dominoes?
Will I sometimes forget to blow my nose?
Will I insist I'm *still* able to drive my car?
Will I end up lost if I wander too far?

Things were much better in *the old days*.
Since then, things have worsened in so many ways.
Will I *keep* thinking back to those much better years?
Will my world be filled with laughter or tears?

Will I still have my teeth? Will I have any hair?
Will I have to endure *personal care?*
Will I be mean or will I be kind?
Will I treat other people as I find?

Will I embrace new technology with the right attitude?
Or go on 'bout *the old days* and just see the good . . .
Not the bad.
Will I be content with the times that I've had?

If my partner dies first, will I live on my own?
Or, if I can't manage, will I live in a home?
Will I shed a tear, as I am doing now
And, to my circumstance, have to bow?

Will I be meek? Will I be proud?
Will I be eccentric or follow the crowd?
Will I relish the wearing of odd socks and loud ties?
Will I go on 'bout *the old days* and how the time flies?

Will I see my relations or rely on the phone?
Will I have lots of friends? Will I just like to moan?
Will I be content in my own company?
If I live till I'm old, how will I be?

Then there's the promise of oncoming heaven
And the prospect of being with loved ones again.
When people meet me . . . what will they see?
Till that new life begins, *that's up to me!*

*Dr Beeching's Report
in 1963 recommended the closure
of a third of the UK railway network. My home town of
Sudbury was one of the affected stations. At that time I was
travelling to school in Colchester on the train. Sudbury was
situated in the middle of the railway line from Cambridge
to Colchester. Despite an active effort to save the line,
the connection to Cambridge was eventually closed and
Sudbury became a terminus. The beautiful station was built
on a curve with an up-line and a down-line and canopies
over both platforms. There was also a pedestrian bridge
connecting the two. The station has sadly since been pulled
down and slightly re-located. It's now just a 'halt' with a tiny
erection like a bus shelter to cower in if it rains.*

*The section between Sudbury and Cambridge gradually fell into decline. I was (and still am) an enthusiastic railway 'nut' and started collecting railway artefacts. British Railways just abandoned all their railway paraphenalia in the various locations. I'd visit the closed stations along the line and would buy items for ten shillings or maybe a pound from the now retired station masters or level crossing keepers. It wasn't long before the whole line looked wild and neglected.*

*This is a lament for the passing of those magnificent steam locomotives and the many railway lines which have been abandoned.*

# No more

No far off whistle blowing loud,
No steam billowing in flowing cloud,
No magnificent creation standing proud,
No more.

No more exciting daring deeds,
No caring 'bout commuter needs,
No more traffic on the lines - just seeds
Blowing in the wind.

No magic . . . as there was before,
Schoolboys no longer stare in awe,
At massive juggernauts of steam - no more.
Their time has gone.

Nature triumphs and reclaims,
No evidence of steam remains,
No sense of urgency, no thrills, no trains . . .

Now stillness reigns.

*At times of tension we tend to recall a time when life was simpler. We seem to forget the horrors of war and re-enactments from different periods of history are now all the rage.*

*My wife and I are enthusiastic 'swing jive' dancers and we particularly look forward to the World War Two Weekend which takes place in October at The North York Moors Railway. We meet up each year and dance on the platform at Grosmont station whilst steam trains arrive and depart on both sides . . . very exciting!*

# The WW2 Weekend

People flock to the World War Weekend.
They put on a costume and go to spend
A few hours in another age, a time of war -
A time we all hoped we'd see no more.

'Digging For Victory' and 'Careless Talk',
Community Singing and The Lambeth Walk,
Kilroy is there and so is Chad -
I remember them all from when I was a lad.

The fur stole, the stocking line,
The Hersche bar, the victory sign,
Mrs Mopp, the spiv in his suit,
And Monty's double who takes the salute.

The old cars, the jeeps, the big guns and the tanks,
The Home Guard, the Tommies, the Jerries and Yanks,
Gas masks and ration books, the women's rolled hair,
The swing jive, the crooners - you'll see them all there.

All reliving the age of steam -
Halcyon days, or so it might seem
But, while romanticism holds its sway,
Old comrades remember a darker day.

Away from the joyfulness of the parade,
They wistfully ponder the price that was paid
And, at eleven o'clock
at the toll of a bell,
They'll sadly
recall that war
was hell.

Yet despite the anxiety it wasn't all bad.
Even then, there were still good times to be had,
For there was a sense of a strong community.
We stood 'gainst the foe, together in unity.

We've lost all that now but at least we don't suffer
Such hardship and poverty. Those days were much tougher.
We shouldn't complain about our lot -
We tend to forget all the things we *have* got.

Let's relive the forties! Come along
And celebrate our hard-won freedom!
Turn that V sign round the other way
And imagine that it's VE Day!

---

*I used to sing in a gospel choir which was full of younger people. We all got on well on the surface but there was a distinct barrier between the generations.*

*Like me, many older people feel it's only their body that has aged and they long to be accepted in a different light.*

# Prime time

In my mind, I'm in my prime.
You see the ravages of time.
You can't see how I used to be.
You don't see the *real* me.

Grey hair, wrinkles, saggy skin,
Just ignore the shape I'm in.
We're opposite ends of a great divide.
Open your mind . . . *see me, inside.*

In my mind, I'm in my prime
But my body's known a better time,
When I could run at twice the speed.
Now I just don't feel the need.

For a while, one of the gang
But then I'm not! I feel a pang
Of envy - sadly you can't see
Inside this shell, a *younger* me.

I'll share a joke, a jape, a jibe
But I'm not a member of your tribe.
I understand . . . you see old age
*But I'm still young within this cage!*

In my mind, I'm in my prime.
What lies between us? Merely time!
The day *may* dawn when you've aged like me
And *then* my point of view you'll see.

When I was young,
I thought like you.
Can I complain if you
share that view?
The time has surely
come for me -
To have to face
reality!

*Cedric and Minnie Fitzwilliam were determined to continue to live their lives to the full. Even so, they often reminisced about the adventures they'd had in their younger days.*

# When Cedric met Min

The Fitzwilliams were planning to celebrate
Forty years of marital bliss
But they'd had no idea what the future would hold
When they stole that first passionate kiss.

Cedric peered at their wedding photo
He thought how little they'd changed,
Though he had to admit
to himself in the end
That some features had
been re-arranged.

His hair had slipped
to the back of his head
And they both were a
little bit wider
He wouldn't be sharing
that thought with Min,
At least, not whilst
sitting beside her.

He laughed when he saw
the clothes he had worn,
Which then were the height
of good taste,
But he had to admit
Min looked stunning
With blonde hair
which reached down
to her waist.

Min's appearance had also seen changes.
Her hair was now curly and grey.
And nowadays if he felt like a cuddle,
Her zimmer frame got in the way!

Now Minnie's real name was Margaret
And that's what it always had been
But her life took a turn for the better
When Cedric arrived on the scene.

In her youth Min was always in trouble,
Full of mischief and cheek and high jinks,
In her red and black, hooped woolly jumper . . .
A dead ringer for Minnie the Minx.

Then Cedric tried hard to remember
How it was that they had first met.
Yes, he'd gone with some friends to the pictures,
Where Min was a young usherette.

In the dark, Cedric took off his blazer.
As he tucked it away on one side,
Loose change fell out of his pockets
And scattered itself far and wide.

His pal Algy, the lad he'd sat next to,
Was startled and gasped "Strike a light".
Cedric, of course, thought he meant it.
In a flash, a Swan Vesta burned bright.

He had to get down on his knees now
Striking matches to help him to see,
Accidentally igniting his 'blazer'
(An appropriate name, now you see).

When Min saw the light she reacted -
She could see just a flame and no more.
Cedric had moved down the row
And was crawling around on the floor.

Thinking fast, she grabbed Cedric's Kia-Ora
With one squirt she extinguished the light.
In the beam of her torch, she saw Cedric -
Their eyes met . . . it was love at first sight!

On that evening *two* flames were ignited.
The pair knew they'd both made a 'catch'.
Their pulses raced - they were excited!
The two made a perfect 'love-match'.

*Postscript from Min:*

An usherette's advice to young maidens
And others still seeking their prince . . .
"I found mine in the dark at the pictures
And I've carried a torch for him since!"

BS/PB

*As I get older I've noticed unwelcome changes to my appearance – hair loss, saggy eyelids, wrinkles and a squarer facial shape. Sometimes I've been surprised when seeing myself in a mirror.*

# On reflection

Who is that staring back at me?
That's not my face, surely, it *can't* be.
It's nothing like my photo on the wall.
He doesn't look like *me* at all.

It can't be me – that's not *my* face.
A stranger must have taken my place
But he does exactly what I do.
When did this happen? It can't be true.

That can't be me – where's my hair?
The top of *his* head's almost bare.
No rugged cheekbone - and look at those jowls.
I stare at him but he just scowls.

Saggy eyelids, bags below,
That's not me - I ought to know.
And what is all that under his chin?
Just look at all that flabby skin!

Where are the rugged looks I had?
That apparition's made me sad.
I can't gaze at that reflection
I've had *enough* of introspection.

The mirror's going to have to go
But what can I do? . . . Yes, I know,
I'll replace it with that framed photo
Of how I *used* to look
     *. . . thirty years ago!*